WRITING

Grade 2

Table of Contents

WRITING

Grade 2

Credits:
McGraw-Hill Children's Publishing Editorial/Production Team
Vincent F. Douglas, B.S. and M. Ed.
Tracey E. Dils
Jennifer Blashkiw Pawley
Teresa A. Domnauer
Tanya Dean
Amy Mayr

Big Tuna Trading Company Art/Editorial/Production Team
Mercer Mayer
John R. Sansevere
Erica Farber
Brian MacMullen
Matthew Rossetti
Linda Hayward
Kamoon Song
Soojung Yoo

 **Children's Publishing**

Send all inquiries to: McGraw-Hill Children's Publishing, 8787 Orion Place, Columbus OH 43240-4027

1-57768-852-X

4 5 6 7 8 9 10 POH 06 05 04 03

WELCOME TO CRITTERVILLE!

Spider

Frog

Grasshopper

Mouse

Little Critter

Little Sister

Dad

Kitty

Mom

Blue

Gator

Bat Child

Gabby

Bun Bun

Tiger

Maurice

Molly

Malcolm

Capitalization

 Remember: Use capital letters for the **names** of

people (or critters)	Gabby	Little Critter	Mr. Rubble
places	Critterville	Snow Hill	Main Street
months	January	April	September
days of the week	Monday	Wednesday	Friday
holidays	Thanksgiving	Fourth of July	Mother's Day

Circle the words below that need a capital letter. Then write each sentence correctly.

On (saturday) my friend, (gabby,) came over.

_____

_____

_____

_____

We made our costumes for the thanksgiving play.

_____

_____

_____

_____

I love november in critterville.

_____

_____

_____

_____

Capitalization

 Remember: Capitalize the first word in a sentence.

We want to eat ice cream.

 Capitalize the main words in a book, movie, or song title.

I am reading a book called How to Find Buried Treasure.

Circle the words below that need a capital letter. Then write each sentence correctly.

the class sang happy birthday to Tiger.

we saw the movie, just a scary monster, on Friday.

did Gabby read the mystery of the missing clue?

End Punctuation

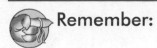

★ Use a period (.) to end a sentence that makes a statement.

> Gator met Little Critter at the bus stop.

★ Use a question mark (?) to end a sentence that asks a question.

> Will they ride the bus today?

★ Use an exclamation point (!) to end a sentence that shows surprise or excitement.

> Watch out!

Little Sister thinks she can put the right punctuation at the end of each sentence. Can you help her? Sure, you can!

Where is Tiger's baseball glove ___

Malcolm has it ___

Oh, no ___

What did Gabby do ___

She found Malcolm's baseball glove ___

Cool ___

Commas in Dates and Places

 Remember: Use commas in dates.

January 23, 2000
December 31, 1999
July 4, 1776

Use commas between the city and state when writing places.

Denver, Colorado
Columbus, Ohio
Albany, New York

Here are some dates and places. Can you put commas where they belong? The first one is done for you.

April 8, 1975   October 16 1937   February 14 2001

Austin Texas   Miami Florida   Boston Massachusetts

Write your birthday on the line below. Put the comma where it belongs.

_____

- -

_____

Write your address on the lines below. On the first line, write your street address. On the second line, write your city and state. Don't forget to use a comma!

_____

- -

_____

- -

_____

Commas in a List

Remember: Use commas for words in a list.

Mom found cookies, marbles, and cars under my pillow.

Add commas to the sentences below. The first one is done for you.

There were clothes, games, and toys in my drawers.

The toy box was full of boats trucks and pajamas.

My sled basketball and snorkel were in the closet.

I keep pebbles crayons and money in my pocket.

All my robots balls and stuffed animals fit under my bed — almost.

Sentences

Remember: A sentence has a **beginning** and an **end**. A sentence tells a complete thought.

These are complete thoughts, so they are sentences:

> Maurice and Molly are twins.
> They like to have fun.

This is not a sentence because it does not tell a complete thought:

> Maurice and Molly

Put these beginnings and endings together to make sentences. Mix them any way you want! Write the sentences on the lines below.

Gator   found a quarter.

After school, Gabby   missed the bus.

Malcolm   won at checkers.

_____

- -

_____

- -

_____

- -

_____

Complete Thoughts: Endings

The sentences below have beginnings, but no endings. Can you finish each sentence so it tells a complete thought? The first one is done for you.

I get so mad when

I lose my pencil.

My best friend and I

My favorite time of the year is

My pet likes to

Someday, I will

Complete Thoughts: Beginnings

The sentences below have endings, but no beginnings. Can you finish each sentence so it tells a complete thought? The first one is done for you.

Noises in the dark

make me really scared.

yesterday.

on my street.

just for Grandma.

in the summer.

Writing Sentences

 Remember: A sentence tells a complete thought.

Little Sister loves to play hopscotch.

Write a sentence about each picture below. Be sure to have a beginning and an ending. Start each sentence with a capital letter and end it with a period.

Sentences in Order

 Remember: The words in a sentence have a special order.

jumps high Grasshopper very

Grasshopper jumps very high.

Put the words in the right order. Be sure each sentence states a complete thought. Begin each sentence with a capital letter and end it with a period.

for toast breakfast eats Malcolm

_____

_____

a Birds eggs lay nest in

_____

_____

has balloon Little Sister a yellow

_____

_____

Writing Statements

 Remember: A sentence that tells you something is called a **statement**. This kind of sentence ends with a **period**.

My dog likes to dig.

Write a statement about each picture below. Begin each sentence with a capital letter and end it with a period.

Just Practicing: All About Me

Little Critter wants to know more about you. Read each question. Then answer each question with a sentence. Don't forget to begin each sentence with a capital letter and end it with a period.

What is your name? (Write **My Name is . . .**) Be sure to write your first, middle, and last names.

_____

- -

_____

Where do you go to school?

_____

- -

_____

What is your favorite holiday?

_____

- -

_____

When is your birthday?

_____

- -

_____

Writing Questions

 Remember: A sentence that asks something is called a **question**. This kind of sentence ends with a **question mark**.

Do you want to play checkers?

Some words that begin a question are: **who, what, when,** and **where.**

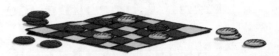

Write a question about each picture below. Begin each question with a capital letter and end it with a question mark.

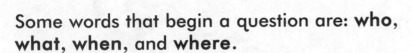

When is your party?

Writing Exclamations

 Remember: An **exclamation** is a sentence that shows excitement or emotion. This kind of sentence ends with an exclamation point.

Cool! Chocolate ice cream!

Oh, no! My dog ate my homework.

Write an exclamation about each picture below. Begin each sentence with a capital letter and end it with an exclamation point.

_____

- - - - - - - - - - - - - - - - - -

_____

_____

- - - - - - - - - - - - - - - - - -

_____

_____

- - - - - - - - - - - - - - - - - -

_____

_____

- - - - - - - - - - - - - - - - - -

_____

_____

- - - - - - - - - - - - - - - - - -

_____

Just Practicing: Statements

Write a statement about each of the things in Mr. Rubble's junkyard.

bird cage

radio

chair

television

tire

Just Practicing: Questions

Little Critter is writing a story about Grandma's prize-winning berry pie. The story will be in the <u>Critterville News</u>. Can you write five questions he can ask Grandma about her pie?

Just Practicing: Exclamations

Little Critter and his friends are at Tiger's surprise party. Can you write five things they might say that are exclamations? You can? Great!

The Five Senses

Can you name the five senses? Your senses help you understand the world around you. Match the pictures of the senses to the correct words.

see

hear

taste

touch

smell

List three things you can see.

_____

- -

_____

List three things you can hear.

_____

- -

Using the Five Senses to Describe

We can write special words to help us describe what we **see**, **hear**, **taste**, **touch**, and **smell**. Draw a line from each describing word to the picture that shows which sense is being used.

shiny

sour

squeaky

sticky

messy

stinky

salty

smooth

purple

buzzing

bumpy

Using Adjectives

Adjectives are describing words that tell us more about something. They make our writing more interesting.

what kind:	blue ribbon	old tire	little house
how many:	three kites	several trees	
how much:	lots of cookies	many bugs	
which one:	that book	those apples	this letter

Little Critter and Su Su both have dogs. Complete each sentence below by writing a describing word (**adjective**) in the blank. Use the word list to help you.

Word List				
funny	smart	yellow	curly	plain
pretty	playful	clean	small	fancy

Little Critter's dog is _____.

Su Su's dog is _____.

Su Su is wearing two _____ bows.

Little Critter is wearing a _____ shirt.

Using Adjectives

 Remember: **Adjectives** are describing words that tell **what kind, how many or how much,** and **which one.**

Look at each picture and write a word that describes it.

Using Adjectives in Sentences

Write a sentence about each picture below. Use at least one adjective in each sentence. Begin each sentence with a capital letter and end it with a period.

Using Adverbs

Adverbs are describing words that tell:

when:	yesterday	soon	now
where:	here	nearby	up
how:	quickly	carefully	happily
to what extent:	very	too	never

Little Critter's friends are having fun, running a race. Complete each sentence below by using a describing word (**adverb**) in the blank. Use the word list to help you.

Word List

slowly	far	today	fast	up
too	very	well	down	soon

Gabby can run _____ .

The race will be over _____ .

Malcolm ran _____ .

He fell _____ .

Little Critter is helping him get _____ .

Using Adverbs in Sentences

 Remember: **Adverbs** are describing words that tell **when, where, how,** and **to what extent.**

Write a sentence about each picture below. Use at least one adverb in each sentence. Begin each sentence with a capital letter and end it with a period. Here are some adverbs to help you, or you can think of your own.

Word List				
just	more	really	several	first
finally	then	fast	here	well

Using Verbs

 Remember: A **verb** is an **action word**.

walk   sing   talk   play

The verb in a sentence tells what is happening. You can use verbs to make your writing clearer and more interesting. Look at how a different verb is used in each sentence below.

Little Sister talked **to Bun Bun.**

Little Sister shouted **at Bun Bun.**

Little Sister whispered **to Bun Bun.**

Here are pairs of verbs. Circle the verb in each pair that describes the action more clearly.

   **walks** **hikes**

   **jumps** **plays**

   **builds** **makes**

   **sees** **finds**

   **gets** **wins**

   **takes** **grabs**

Using Verbs in Sentences

Write your own sentences below. Choose the word from each pair that describes the action more clearly.

bends   bows

_____

- - - - - - - - - - - - - - - - -

_____

moves   kicks

_____

- - - - - - - - - - - - - - - - -

_____

touches   chops

_____

- - - - - - - - - - - - - - - - -

_____

taps   punches

_____

- - - - - - - - - - - - - - - - -

_____

shouts   says

_____

- - - - - - - - - - - - - - - - -

_____

Comparisons with -er and -est

Sometimes you may need to describe something by comparing it to another thing. In this case, you may use the endings -er and -est.

The ending -er is used when comparing two things.
The ending -est is used when comparing three or more things.

Dad is tall.   **Dad is taller.**   **Dad is the tallest.**

Write the correct describing word on each line below.

Malcolm is _____.

      strong   stonger   the strongest

Grasshopper is _____.

      small   smaller   the smallest

Gator swims _____.

      fast   faster   the fastest

Bun Bun jumps _____.

      high   higher   the highest

Comparisons with **more** and **most**

When you use a big word to compare one thing to another thing, you need to use the words **more** or **most**.

More is used when comparing two things.
Most is used when comparing three or more things.

This gift is wonderful. This gift is more wonderful. This gift is the most wonderful.

Write the correct describing word on each line below.

That picture is _____.

colorful   more colorful   the most colorful

That maze is _____.

difficult   more difficult   the most difficult

This pie is _____.

delicious   more delicious   the most delicious

That teddy bear is _____.

expensive   more expensive   the most expensive

Comparisons with **like** or **as**

Another way to compare two things is to use **like** or **as**.

She sings. Birds sing.
So you can write:

She sings like a bird.

The cookie is sweet. Honey is sweet.
So you can write:

The cookie is as sweet as honey.

Complete the sentences using clues from the pictures and the words below.

bunny	hungry	soft
teakettle	horse	baby

Her coat is as _____ as a _____.

Little Critter whistled like a _____.

Tiger is as _____ as a _____.

Little Sister cried like a _____.

Comparisons with **like** or **as**

Use the word list to fill in the blanks in these comparisons. Write the sentences on the lines below.

Word List			
twinkle	swim	pillow	sticky
soft	stars	tape	fish

I can _____ like a _____.

The floor is as _____ as _____.

Her eyes _____ like _____.

My doll is as _____ as a _____.

Writing Descriptive Sentences

Look around at all the fun that's going on. Can you write five descriptive sentences about what you see? Be sure to begin each sentence with a capital letter and end it with a period. Use describing words, comparisons, and verbs to make your sentences interesting.

Describing People

You can use lots of describing words when you write about people. Think about how the person **looks**. Describe the person's (or critter's) size, hair, and clothes.

Bat Child is short.
He has big, brown wings.
His ears stand straight up.
He wears a yellow shirt and
    purple pants.

Look at the describing words above. Can you think of more describing words for the critters below? Write at least three describing words (for each critter) on the lines below.

Describing People

Here are some words you can use when describing a person, his or her clothes, and his or her hair.

Draw a person in the box below. Then write four sentences that describe the person. You may use the word list to help you.

Word List

tall	curly	large
round	fuzzy	small
thin	straight	striped
short	dark	dotted
medium	light	plain
strong	long	silly

Writing Riddles

A fun way to practice using words that describe is to write a **riddle**. A riddle is a puzzle. You must read the description and then try to guess what the thing is that is being described. Here is an example:

I keep things safe.
I have a hole in my middle.
A key will open me.
Can you guess what I am?

I am a lock.

Read each of the riddles below and guess what is being described.

I know the numbers 1 through 12.
I have two hands.
My hands move all day long.
Can you guess what I am?

_____

I am a _____.

My name is the same as what I do.
People try to swat at me.
Can you guess what I am?

_____

I am a _____.

I lay around all the time.
Everyone steps on me, but it doesn't hurt.
Dogs like to sleep on me.
Can you guess what I am?

_____

I am a _____.

Writing Riddles

You can write riddles, too! Look at the pictures below. Write a riddle for each object, using the describing words in the box. Or, you can use your own describing words.

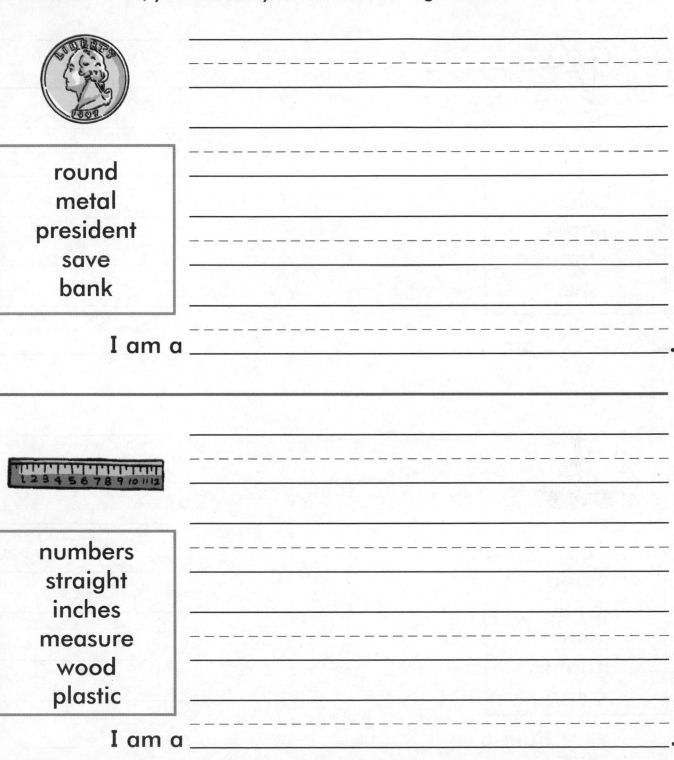

round
metal
president
save
bank

I am a _____.

numbers
straight
inches
measure
wood
plastic

I am a _____.

Writing More Riddles

Keep practicing! Making up riddles will help you use interesting words in all your writing!

tail
wind
paper
string
fly

I am a _____ .

hot
wood
cook
glow
bright
camp

I am a _____ .

Just Practicing: My Family and Me

Draw a picture of your family in the box below. Then use describing words to tell all about you and your family.

My Family and Me

Just Practicing: All About My Stuff

Draw a picture of your favorite stuff: toys, books, sports things — whatever you like to play with or collect. Then use describing words to tell all about your stuff.

All About My Stuff

_____

- - - - - - - - - - - - - - - - - -

_____

- - - - - - - - - - - - - - - - - -

_____

- - - - - - - - - - - - - - - - - -

_____

- - - - - - - - - - - - - - - - - -

_____

- - - - - - - - - - - - - - - - - -

_____

- - - - - - - - - - - - - - - - - -

_____

- - - - - - - - - - - - - - - - - -

The Writing Process

The Writing Process is a set of steps to help you make your writing the best it can be. Read about the Writing Process below. You'll get to try each step on your own in the pages that follow.

1 Prewriting

Prewriting is what you do before you write. It is a way of collecting your thoughts and ideas for what you want to write about. Sometimes it is called **brainstorming**.

2 Drafting

Your first try at a piece of writing is called a **rough draft**. When you write a rough draft, don't worry about spelling and punctuation — just get your writing started!

3 Revising

Revising means making corrections. When you revise your writing, you want to be sure it makes sense. You want to make sure nothing is missing. This is also a good time to check that you have used interesting words.

4 Proofreading

When you **proofread** your writing, you are looking for mistakes. Now, it is time to check your spelling, punctuation, and to make sure you capitalized words correctly.

5 Publishing

When you **publish** your writing, you are ready for people to read it! You should use your best handwriting and a nice clean piece of paper. Or, you can type what you have written on a computer.

Prewriting

The first step of the writing process is called prewriting.
Pre- means **before**, so **prewriting** means **before writing.**

This is the time when you get to think about writing. Here are some questions you can ask yourself when you are prewriting:

- **What do I want to write about?**
- **What do I know a lot about?**
- **Where can I find information?**
- **What are some words or ideas I can use for my topic?**

Now let's practice doing some prewriting!

One fun topic to write about is ANIMALS. Can you answer these prewriting questions about ANIMALS? Write down whatever you think of.

What animals do I want to write about?

_____

_____

What animal do I know a lot about?

_____

_____

What are some words or ideas about that animal?

_____

_____

Where can I find more information about that animal?

_____

_____

Prewriting — Brainstorming

One way to prewrite is to brainstorm.

Brainstorming means thinking of everything you can think of about a topic. Then you write down each idea.

You will make a list of words and ideas about your topic. There are no right or wrong words, or good or bad ideas. Just write whatever comes into your brain.

Here's a topic to brainstorm. Little Critter has started a list. Can you add lots of your own words and ideas?

A Day at the Beach

sand	playing	big waves
water	finding stuff	

Prewriting — Writing Webs

Another prewriting method is **writing webs**, also called story webs or clustering. Again, you think of everything you can about a topic. Then you write each idea down like this:

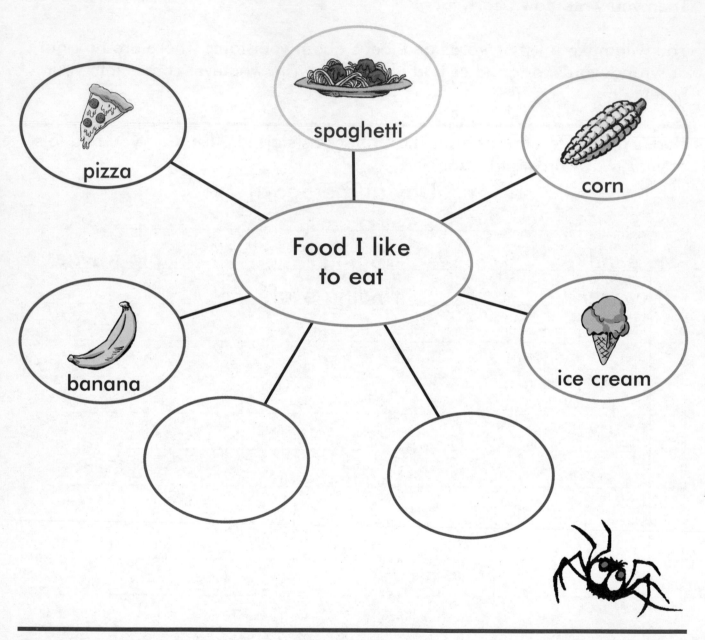

Can you add two more ideas to this web?

Prewriting — Writing Webs

Here is a topic for you. Can you fill in the web with words and ideas that you could write about?

Things my friends and I like to do

Prewriting — Freewriting

Another kind of prewriting is called **freewriting**. It is just what it sounds like. You are **free** to **write** whatever comes to mind.

You just start writing and keep going. Don't worry about what fits. Don't worry about spelling or capitals or punctuation. You can fix all that later.

Freewriting helps your ideas come out! Just write . . . and write . . . and write!

Little Critter did some freewriting. Read what he wrote, and then answer the question below.

I like animals. I have a goldfish. Mom says I am responsible for her. She lives in a goldfish bowl. She likes to swim. I like to swim, too. Sometimes I forget to feed her. But Mom reminds me.

Can you figure out what Little Critter's topic was?

_____

– –

_____

Just Practicing: Brainstorming

Here are some topics that Gabby and Little Critter like to write about. Pick one topic and do your own **brainstorming** below.

My Vacation
Just Me and My Dog
Going to the Fair
When I Grow Up
A Job I Did

Title: _____

Just Practicing: Writing Webs

Now it's time for you to make your own writing web. First, choose your topic. What kinds of things do you know a lot about? Gator has some ideas to get you started.

dinosaurs	**planets**	**magic tricks**
on the farm	**car games**	**places to go**

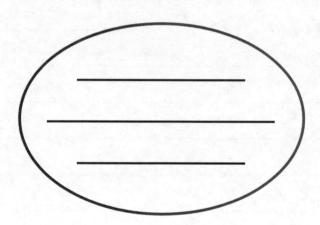

Just Practicing: Freewriting

Now it's time for you to do your own freewriting. Choose a topic from the pictures you see. Then write, write, write — whatever you think of about that topic.

Just Practicing: Prewriting Your Way

Which kind of prewriting do you like best?

brainstorming

writing webs

freewriting

Use whichever kind of prewriting you want as you prewrite about:

My Very Best Day at School

Drafting

Step two of the writing process is called **drafting.** It is time to take all of the ideas and words you came up with during prewriting and begin to write the real thing.

Let's practice using this topic: **Going to the Farm.**

Start by doing some prewriting. What do you see in the pictures? What do you know about going to a farm?

Drafting

Now it's time to write a draft. Look at all of the ideas you have about **Going to the Farm**. Which ones go together? Take the ideas and words and make complete sentences.

Example: cows, chickens, horses, goats

Now write some sentences using your ideas from page 53.

_____

- -

_____

- -

_____

- -

_____

- -

_____

- -

_____

- -

_____

Just Practicing: Rough Draft

All of the sentences you **drafted** on page 54 can be put in order to make a story. Can you put your sentences together so your story makes sense? Try it on the lines below.

Revising

After drafting, it is time for step three of the writing process: **revising**. To revise means **to change**.

Look closely at what you have written. You can ask yourself questions such as:

- Does this make sense?
- Have I used interesting words?
- Am I missing anything?
- Does everything belong here?
- Should I take something out?
- Do I have things in a good order?

Revise the sentences until you have a better story. Don't worry about spelling, punctuation, or capitals yet. That will come next.

Look at the sentences below. Revise each one to make it a more interesting sentence. Then draw a line to the number to show which sentence should come first, second, and third.

After school, I did something.

_____

- -

_____

1

That night, I read something.

_____

- -

_____

2

Before school, I ate something.

_____

- -

_____

3

Attention writers! Sometimes you will revise more than once before a sentence or story is really terrific.

Just Practicing: Revising

 Remember: When you **revise**, ask yourself these questions:

- Does this make sense?
- Have I used interesting words?
- Am I missing anything?
- Does everything belong here?
- Should I take something out?
- Do I have things in a good order?

Look at the story you wrote on page 55. Revise it on the lines below.

_____

_____

_____

_____

_____

_____

_____

_____

_____

How does your story look now? Is it better?

Show your story to a parent or teacher. Does he or she have any ideas to help you revise it even more?

Proofreading

Is your story better now? If you need to revise it more, use another piece of paper.

When you are finished revising, it is time for step four of the writing process: **proofreading**.

Now you can fix mistakes in

- spelling
- punctuation
- capitalization

Here are some proofreading marks that will help you. See how they are used in the story below.

Proofreading Marks

⬭	misspelling
≡	make a capital letter
⊙	add a period
?	add a question mark

I went to schoool yesterday. I forgot my books⊙They

were at home. Why did I forget them? My dog, blue, was

sleeping on then miss kitty didn't

scold me. She was really nice to

mee Maybe Miss Kitty has a dog

at her house, to

Proofreading

It is time to practice **proofreading**.

Remember: You are looking for mistakes in:

- **spelling**   I caught (for) fish.

- **punctuation**   Wait! You can't go there⊙

- **capitalization** m̲i̲ss k̲i̲tty has a dog

                        at home.

The proofreading marks are here to help you.

Proofreading Marks
◯ misspelling
≡   make a capital letter
⊙   add a period
!   add an exclamation point
?   add a question mark

Proofread the following sentences.

It's lunch time! We have fun eeting our lunch with Bat

child. he does magick tricks for us Wow Look at how he

makes my spoon disappear

Can he make it come back

I sure hope so. I want to eat

my pudding.

Proofread these sentences, too.

The critterville team has a game on tusday.

Who are they playing   We want too go watch tham.

Let's go, together. Meet me at twevle o'clock.

Just Practicing: Proofreading

The more you practice **proofreading**, the better your writing will be.

Practice by proofreading the sentences below. Write the corrected sentences on the lines.

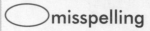

Proofreading Marks

◯ misspelling

≡   make a capital letter

⊙   add a period

!   add an exclamation point

?   add a question mark

I slept in a tent wen we went camping

_____

_____

Did you see me mak a home run

_____

_____

My freinds and I had fun in our clubhouse

_____

_____

There was a pudle next to my dog

_____

_____

Will you read me a storie about super critter

_____

_____

Publishing

 Remember: Step five of the writing process is called **publishing**.

There are lots of ways to publish your writing. Look at the examples below.

How would you publish your writing?

Proofreading and Publishing

Now go back to your story on page 57. Read what you wrote. Proofread your story for mistakes.

Now write the **final draft** on the lines below.

_____

- -

_____

- -

_____

- -

_____

- -

_____

- -

_____

- -

_____

Step five of the writing process is called publishing.

It happens when your writing is finished. You have fixed the mistakes. You have written or typed your story neatly. Now it is ready for others to read.

Show your story to a friend, to a parent, or to a teacher. When you have done all of these things, you have published your writing!

My Summer Vacation

  Remember: The writing process is made of these steps:

Step One
Prewriting

Step Two
Drafting

Step Three
Revising

Step Four
Proofreading

Step Five
Publishing

You can use the following pages to write a story about your summer vacation — a real one or an imaginary one.
Start on this page. You can do brainstorming or a writing web or freewriting. Put your prewriting here.

My Summer Vacation

My Summer Vacation

Use your prewriting to go to the next step: **drafting.** Use your ideas to write complete sentences. This is your draft.

My Summer Vacation

_____

- -

_____

- -

_____

- -

_____

- -

_____

- -

_____

- -

_____

- -

_____

- -

_____

- -

_____

My Summer Vacation

Read your first draft. How can you make it better? It is time to go to the next step: **revising.** If you need to, go back to page 56 and look at the questions you can ask yourself as you revise. Write your new draft below.

My Summer Vacation

_____
- -
_____
_____
- -
_____
_____
- -
_____
_____
- -
_____
_____
- -
_____
_____
- -
_____
_____
- -

Now, read your draft. It is time for proofreading. Use the proofreading marks to fix the mistakes.

Then write your story without the mistakes on the next page. Be sure to let someone read it!

My Summer Vacation

My Summer Vacation
by

_____

_____

(your name)

_____

_____

_____

_____

_____

_____

_____

_____

_____

The Main Idea

The **main idea** tells what a story is mostly about. Every story has a main idea.

Here is an example:

Little Critter gets a haircut.

Look at the pictures below. Put a check mark (✓) in front of the best main idea for each picture.

_____ Sports are fun.

_____ Three friends have a contest.

_____ Gabby can jump.

_____ Dogs make good pets.

_____ The dog is ready to play.

_____ Dogs like to bury things.

The Main Idea

 Remember: The **main idea** tells what a picture or story is mostly about.

Write the main idea for each picture below. Be sure to write a complete sentence. Start with a capital letter and end with a period.

_____

_____

_____

_____

_____

_____

_____

_____

_____

Writing a Title

The name of a picture or story is called a **title**. The title tells the main idea.

Here is an example:

Super Critter to the Rescue

Look at the pictures below. Put a check mark (✓) in front of the best title for each picture.

_____ **Little Sister Loves Summer**

_____ **Little Sister Plays in the Pool**

_____ **Little Sister Wants Summer to Come**

_____ **Grandpa Has a New Hat**

_____ **Grandpa Wants to Fish**

_____ **Grandpa Goes Fishing**

Writing a Title

 Remember: The **title** is the name of the story or picture.

Write a title for each picture below. Be sure to use capital letters for the important words.

Story Parts

Every story has a **beginning**, a **middle**, and an **end**.

beginning

Gator collected rocks.

middle

He sorted the rocks.

end

He made a display.

Draw lines to show which picture is the beginning, which is the middle, and which is the end.

beginning

beginning

middle

middle

end

end

Story Parts

 Remember: Every story has a **beginning**, a **middle**, and an **end**.

Can you fill in the beginning, middle, and end of this story? Write sentences to complete the story.

Planting Vegetables

Beginning

_____

- - - - - - - - - - - - - - - - - - -

_____

- - - - - - - - - - - - - - - - - - -

_____

Middle

_____

- - - - - - - - - - - - - - - - - - -

_____

- - - - - - - - - - - - - - - - - - -

_____

End

_____

- - - - - - - - - - - - - - - - - - -

_____

_____

- - - - - - - - - - - - - - - - - - -

Setting — Place

Every story has a setting. The **setting** is the **place** where the story happens.

You will need to describe the setting so your reader can "see" it.

Here is an example:

Dad and I went camping. Our campsite was really cool. We were surrounded by lots of big, leafy trees. We pitched our tent near a huge rock. The lake was so close we could see it from our tent. We used branches and twigs on the ground for our campfire. That night it was so dark, I could see a zillion stars in the sky. It was great out there — just the campfire, my dad, and me!

Can you "see" the place that Little Critter is telling about? Underline all of the words that describe the setting.

Setting — Time

The setting is the place where the story happens. But the **setting** is also the **time** in which the story happens.

Your reader needs to know when the story is happening.

Look again at this example:

Dad and I went camping. Our campsite was really cool. We were surrounded by lots of big, leafy trees. We pitched our tent near a huge rock. The lake was so close we could see it from our tent. We used branches and twigs on the ground for our campfire. That night it was so dark, I could see a zillion stars in the sky. It was great out there — just the campfire, my dad, and me!

Can you find the words that describe the time of day? Underline all of the words that describe the time this story is about.

Just Practicing: Setting — Place

Remember: The **setting** includes the **place** where the story happens.

Think of a place that you know well. It could be a room, your neighborhood, a special place you visited, or an imaginary place.

Brainstorm some words and ideas about that place. Think about what you **see, hear, smell, taste,** or **feel** in that place.

Place: _____

Just Practicing: Setting — Time

Now add the other part of **setting: time**.

Go back to page 75. Add sentences that describe the time. Time can be

- time of day
- a holiday
- season of the year
- a time in history
- a time in the future

It answers the question: When is this story happening?

Read the following story. Then answer the questions below.

It was getting dark. The wind blew against my face. I felt snowflakes hit my nose. I put my hood up over my head. I looked up at a clock in a store window. In fifteen minutes, it would be suppertime.

What time of day is it?

_____

_____

What season of the year is it?

_____

_____

What is the weather like?

_____

_____

Just Practicing:
Setting — Place and Time

Gator wants to write a story about what happened when he went rock collecting in the desert. What are some words he can use to describe the setting?

Place	**Time**

Just Practicing:
Setting — Place and Time

Gabby wants to write a story about what happened on Snow Hill last weekend. What are some words she can use to describe the setting?

Place	Time

My Room

Little Critter wants to know what your room looks like. Can you write some sentences that describe what it is like to be in your room?

Think of describing words. What do you **see**, **hear**, **smell**, **taste**, or **feel** when you are in your room?

Prewriting space: Brainstorming, writing a web, or freewriting? You choose!

My Room

Look at the describing words you wrote on page 79. Now write sentences using some of the words.
Write your draft below.

Creative Writing

Characters

The people (or animals or critters) the story is about are the **characters.** Every story has at least one character. The character may even be you!

The reader of the story needs to "see" the characters. It is important to describe each one. There are lots of things to tell about when describing a character:

age	young	grown-up	teenager
size	short	skinny	large
clothes	neat	comfortable	messy
features (hair, eyes, mouth, etc.)	curly	dark	smiling
personality	kind	silly	shy
mood	nervous	tired	happy

Look at the picture below and write three words to describe the character.

_____

_ _ _ _ _ _ _ _ _ _ _ _ _ _ _ _ _ _ _ _

_____

_ _ _ _ _ _ _ _ _ _ _ _ _ _ _ _ _ _ _ _

_____

_ _ _ _ _ _ _ _ _ _ _ _ _ _ _ _ _ _ _ _

_____

Characters

 Remember: A **character** is someone who the story is about. Can you write three words to describe each character below?

_____

- - - - - - - - - - - - - - -

_____

- - - - - - - - - - - - - - -

_____

- - - - - - - - - - - - - - -

_____

- - - - - - - - - - - - - - -

_____

- - - - - - - - - - - - - - -

_____

- - - - - - - - - - - - - - -

Characters

What if you were the **character** in your story? Can you describe yourself? Start by drawing a picture of yourself.

Now write some sentences that describe YOU.

Characters and Setting

Read the story below. <u>Underline</u> all of the words that describe the **character**. Then circle all of the words that describe the **setting**.

A Day at the Playground

Blue and I had all day to play. Blue is my spotted dog.

We went to the playground near the school. I wore my old,

blue overalls and my striped shirt. Blue wore his red collar.

The playground was empty. We could play on the big slide

without waiting in line. Blue dug a few holes in the sand.

Then we raced to the new yellow bench and back again.

We had fun!

Dialogue

When characters talk, the words they say are called **dialogue**. Writing dialogue is easy, but you need to use special punctuation.

"Let's go to the clubhouse," said Gabby.

Little Critter answered, "Okay with me!"

The words a character speaks are put in quotation marks ("").

You separate the dialogue ("Let's go to the clubhouse") from the information about who is speaking (said Gabby) with a comma (,).

Put in the correct punctuation in the sentences below. The first one has been done for you.

"Here's some jelly for our sandwiches," said Molly.

Maurice said   I'll get the peanut butter.

Mom told Dad   Little Sister needs new shoes.

We can go shopping tomorrow   he answered.

Dialogue

 Remember: The words characters say are called **dialogue**.

Sometimes dialogue is a question and uses a question mark (?).

"Who is ready for dessert?" asked Mom.

Mom asked, "Who is ready for dessert?"

And sometimes dialogue is an exclamation and uses an exclamation point (!).

"Watch out!" cried Tiger.

Tiger cried, "Watch out!"

Put in the correct punctuation in the sentences below.

Where is my glove   asked Tiger.

Did you lose it   asked Gator.

Little Critter asked,   Do you want to play

Gabby yelled,   Be careful

Thanks   Maurice and Molly yelled back.

Writing Dialogue

Now you can write some **dialogue**. Think of what you want Dad and Little Critter to say to each other. Then fill in the dialogue on the lines below.

" _____ "
_____ ,

said Dad. _____

" _____ "
_____ ,

said Little Critter. _____

" _____ "
_____ ,

said Dad. _____

Just Practicing: Writing Dialogue

What are these characters saying to each other? Write the dialogue below.

_____

- -

_____

- -

_____

_____

- -

_____

- -

_____

The Problem

An interesting story usually has a **problem** that needs to be solved. Describe the problem in the pictures below.

Problem:

Malcolm is going too fast.

Problem:

_____

Problem:

_____

The Solution

Now that we have a problem, we need to solve the problem. The answer to a problem is called a **solution**. Describe a way to solve each problem in the pictures below. Be creative! Use your imagination.

Solution:

Malcolm should slow down.

Solution:

_____

Solution:

_____

The Problem and the Solution

Now, make up your own problem and solution. Draw a picture of your problem and solution and describe them below.

Problem:

Solution:

Setting, Characters, and the Problem

 Remember:

- The place and time in a story is the **setting**.
- The people a story is about are the **characters**.
- The problem in a story is the **conflict**.

Read the story below. Then answer the questions about setting, characters, and conflict on the next page.

After lunch, the sun was covered by lots of clouds. Little Sister and I knew it was going to rain. We sat by the window and watched the sky get darker and darker.

Soon rain was falling and the wind was blowing. Little Sister looked scared. She doesn't like storms. I told her it would be okay. Then we heard loud thunder. The lights went out. Little Sister crawled under the table. Soon she was fast asleep.

When she woke up, the storm was over. I am glad she didn't see all the lightning! It was scary!

Setting, Characters, and the Problem

Who are the characters in the story?

_____

_____

_____

What is the setting of the story? (time and place)

_____

_____

_____

What are some words used to describe the setting?

_____

_____

_____

What is the problem in the story?

_____

_____

_____

Picture Stories — Comics

Do you like to read comics? So does Little Critter! He reads them every day! Sometimes he likes to draw them, too.

Comics are stories, too. They use setting and characters — and there's usually a problem.

Who are the **characters** in Little Critter's comic strip?

_____

- -

_____

- -

_____

What is the **setting?**

_____

- -

_____

- -

_____

What is the **problem?**

_____

- -

_____

Picture Stories — Comics

Can you draw your own comic strip? Be sure to write what the characters are saying to each other. Think about the setting, characters, and a problem.

Who are the characters in your comic strip?

_____

_____

_____

_____

What is the setting?

_____

_____

_____

_____

What is the problem?

_____

_____

_____

_____

Just Practicing: Comics

Here is another place for you to create a comic strip! Have fun!

Who are the **characters** in your comic strip?

_____

_____

_____

What is the **setting**?

_____

_____

_____

What is the **problem**?

_____

_____

_____

Just Practicing: Story Starters

Here is a story that Little Critter started to write. Finish the story on the lines below. Begin by describing the setting.

When I woke up, I looked out the window and saw . . .

_____

_____

_____

_____

_____

_____

_____

_____

_____

_____

_____

_____

_____

_____

_____

_____

_____

_____

Just Practicing: Story Starters

Here is the beginning of another story. As you finish writing it, add some dialogue.

I was so mad when . . .

_____

- -

_____

- -

_____

- -

_____

- -

_____

- -

_____

- -

_____

- -

_____

- -

_____

- -

Just Practicing: Story Starters

Finish the story that Gabby started below. Think of a problem to make the story interesting.

One day last summer, my dad and I went . . .

_____

_____

_____

_____

_____

_____

_____

_____

_____

_____

_____

_____

_____

_____

_____

_____

Journal Writing

A **journal** is a special book for your own writing. It is a kind of diary.

There are no rules about writing in a journal. Here are some ideas to help you learn about journal writing.

- You can write every day or just when you want to.
- You can write whatever you want: stories, poems, "what I did today," or anything!
- No one has to read your journal but you.
- You can write, draw, or paste in stuff you want to keep.
- It helps if you put the date on the page when you write. Then you will know when you wrote that page.

Look at a page in Little Critter's journal. This is what he wrote last summer:

> ### July 4, 2001
>
> Today is the Fourth of July. We had a picnic in our backyard. Grandma and Grandpa came. Dad cooked stuff on the grill. Mom made fresh corn and fruit salad.
>
> But the best part was at night. We saw lots of fireworks! They were big and bright. And loud! Little Sister put her hands over her ears. But I didn't. I liked the loud noise. I laughed and laughed.

Just Practicing: Journal Writing

Write your own journal entry on the lines below. Write about anything you want. Be sure to put a date at the top of the entry.

Just Practicing: A Pirate's Journal

Pretend that you are a pirate who just found a buried treasure. Write a journal entry about it! Choose a date from long ago to put at the top of the entry.

Just Practicing: My Autobiography

An **autobiography** is the story of the life of the person who writes it.

Some things to include in your **autobiography** are:

- when you were born
- where you were born
- information about your family:
  their names, relationships, etc.
- places you have lived
- things you have done

Think about those things. Then use the space below to prewrite ideas you want to include in your autobiography. You can brainstorm, use writing webs, or freewrite.

Just Practicing: My Autobiography

 Remember: Your autobiography is the story of your life written by you. Use the space below to **draft** your autobiography. Write complete sentences.

All About Me

Just Practicing: My Autobiography

Use the space below to **revise** the draft of your autobiography. Ask yourself:

- Am I missing anything?
- Do I have everything in good order?
- Should I take anything out?
- Does everything belong here?
- Have I used interesting verbs and describing words?

All About Me

_____

_____

_____

_____

_____

_____

_____

_____

_____

_____

_____

_____

_____

_____

_____

_____

_____

Just Practicing: My Autobiography

Go back to page 105 and **proofread** what you have written. Look for mistakes in spelling, capitalization, and punctuation. Then write your **final draft** below.

All About Me

_____

- -

_____

- -

_____

- -

_____

- -

_____

- -

_____

- -

_____

- -

_____

- -

_____

- -

_____

To **publish** your autobiography, just let someone read all about you!

What Is a Paragraph?

A **paragraph** is a group of sentences that are about the same idea. Read the paragraph below.

Little Critter knows how to take good care of his dog, Blue. He gives Blue fresh food and water every day. He takes his dog out for walks so that Blue can get exercise. He brushes Blue's fur once a day and gives him a bath once a week. When Blue is not feeling well, Little Critter takes him to the vet. With such good care, Blue stays happy and healthy, and that makes Little Critter happy, too!

Look at the paragraph again. Circle the sentence that tells what the paragraph is mostly about.

Did you circle this sentence?

Little Critter knows how to take good care of his dog, Blue.

If you did, you are right! The first sentence in a paragraph usually tells what the paragraph is mostly about. This is called the **topic sentence**. The rest of the sentences in the paragraph tell about how Little Critter takes good care of his dog.

What Belongs and What Doesn't Belong

 Remember: A **paragraph** is a group of sentences about the **same idea**.

Look at the paragraph below. Some of the sentences do not belong. They are underlined.

Little Critter knows how to take good care of his dog, Blue. He gives Blue fresh food and water every day. <u>One day, Little Critter forgot to turn off the water.</u> He takes his dog out for walks so that Blue can get exercise. He brushes Blue's fur once a day and gives him a bath once a week. <u>Mrs. Critter made a red sweater for Blue.</u> With such good care, Blue stays happy and healthy, and that makes Little Critter happy, too!

When you find a sentence that does not go with the paragraph topic sentence, you should take it out. Underline the sentences in the paragraph below that do not belong.

Making an ice cream cone is easy. First, get the ice cream from the freezer. Mom bought some frozen juice, too! Next, get a cone and an ice cream scoop. Now scoop out some ice cream from the container. Chocolate is my favorite flavor. Put the ice cream on the cone. You're all done!

Writing Paragraphs

Now, look at the paragraph on page 107 again.

Did you notice that the first sentence does not line up with the other sentences? It starts a little over to the right. That is called **indenting**. You should always **indent** the first sentence in a paragraph.

Finish writing the paragraph below. The **topic sentence** is written for you. Notice that it is **indented**!

Don't forget that the sentences you add must be about the **topic sentence**.

I know how to help my mom and dad. _____

_____

_____

_____

_____

_____

_____

_____

_____

_____

_____

Just Practicing: Writing Paragraphs

Here is another **paragraph** for you to complete. Make sure all of your sentences are about the **topic sentence** below.

There are lots of ways to earn money.

Just Practicing: Writing Paragraphs

Now, write your own paragraph about the picture below.
Remember:

- **Indent** the first sentence of your paragraph.
- Your first sentence is usually your **topic sentence**.
  It tells what the paragraph is mostly about.
- All the sentences that follow should be about your topic sentence.

Using Order Words

When you write a paragraph, you need to make the order of events clear. Using **order words** will help.
Here are some order words you can use.

first	next	now	finally
second	then	later	last

Look at the pictures below. Label each picture in order. Use these words:

first **next** **last**

_____ ___first___ _____

Look at the pictures below. Label each picture in order. Use these words:

first **then** **finally**

_____ _____ _____

Using Order Words

 Remember: Using **order words** makes your writing clearer.

Read the paragraph below. Without order words, this paragraph is not clear. Write an order word in each of the blanks. Use the list on page 112 to help you.

Bun Bun wants to send out birthday party invitations.

_____ she will make a list of her friends.

_____ she will write her name on each invitation.

_____ she will write the date and time of the

party. _____ Bun Bun will address each envelope

and put on a stamp. _____ she will go to the post

office and put the invitations in the mailbox. The invitations

are on their way!

Just Practicing: Using Order Words

Use **order words** when you write the following paragraph.
Be sure to **indent** the first sentence.

How to Make Little Critter's Favorite Sandwich

_____

_____

_____

_____

_____

_____

_____

_____

_____

_____

_____

_____

_____

_____

Parts of a Friendly Letter

Friendly letters are fun to write. It's nice to send letters to friends and relatives. And it's great to get a letter, too. There are rules about writing letters. Every letter is made of these parts.

> **The date** must go at the top right side of the letter.

> The letter begins with a **greeting**, usually **Dear**, and the name of the person. Always put a comma at the end.

> The main part of a letter is called the **body**.

> The letter ends with a **closing**. You can write **Yours truly** or **Sincerely**. The first word is capitalized. Always put a comma at the end of the closing.

> The writer signs his or her name at the bottom. This is called the **signature**.

April 6, 2002

Dear Bun Bun,

    I had fun at your birthday party on Saturday. The cake was good and the games were fun. I liked the party favors, too. Thanks for inviting me.

Your friend,
Little Critter

What is the main part of a letter called? _____

Where do you put the date? _____

What do you call the "Dear . . ." part? _____

What do you call the "Yours truly" part? _____

Parts of a Friendly Letter

Can you label the parts of a friendly letter? Put these words where they go in the boxes below.

signature   greeting   date   closing   body

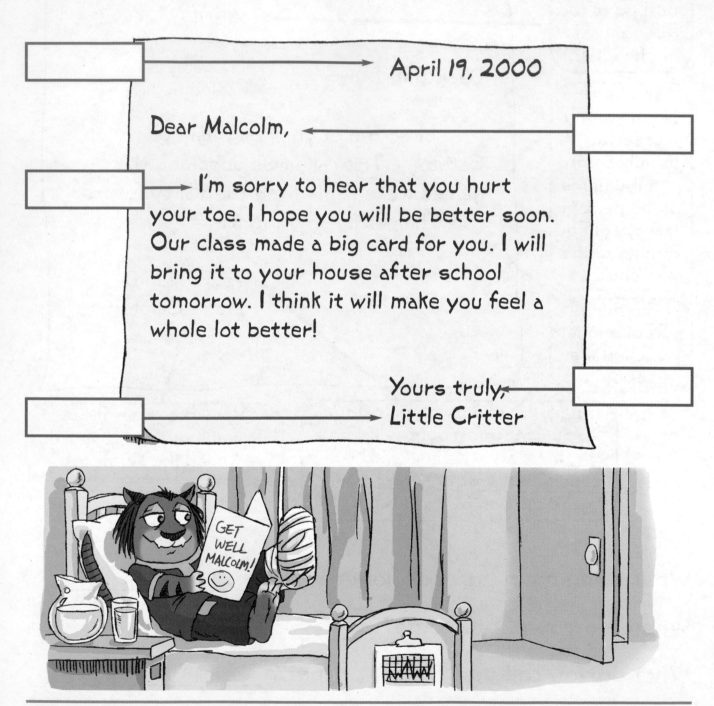

April 19, 2000

Dear Malcolm,

I'm sorry to hear that you hurt your toe. I hope you will be better soon. Our class made a big card for you. I will bring it to your house after school tomorrow. I think it will make you feel a whole lot better!

Yours truly,
Little Critter

Attention writers: Paragraphs are indented in letters, too!

Just Practicing: Writing a Friendly Letter

Mr. Rubble let Little Critter have a piece of junk from the junkyard. Now Little Critter wants to write him and tell him what he did with it.

Pretend you are Little Critter and write a letter to Mr. Rubble. Some parts of the letter are filled in to help you. (Hint: Look back at page 19 to see things in Mr. Rubble's Junkyard.)

_____ ,
(date)

<u>Dear</u> _____ ,
(greeting)

I _____

_____

_____

_____
(body)

_____

_____

_____

_____

<u>Sincerely,</u>
(closing)

<u>Little Critter</u>
(signature)

Just Practicing: Writing a Friendly Letter

Tiger just won a karate match. He wants to write a letter to his cousin about the match.

Pretend you are Tiger and write a letter to your cousin. Make sure to use commas in the date, the greeting, and the closing. (Hint: Look at page 30 to see Tiger practicing karate.)

_____

_____

_____

_____

_____

_____

_____

_____

_____

_____

_____

Just Practicing: Writing a Thank You Note

A **thank you note** is like a friendly letter. You include all of the same parts: **date, greeting, body, closing,** and **signature.** But it is special because it is written for one reason: to thank someone for something.

Gabby's aunt sent her a new book — <u>The Haunted Cave Mystery</u>. Gabby wants to thank her for it. Pretend you are Gabby and write a thank you note to your aunt. Look back at page 115 if you need help.

Writing an Invitation

An **invitation** is a short note with one purpose: to ask someone to come to something, like a birthday party, wedding, or other celebration.

An invitation must give information about:

- **what** the event is
- **who** the event is for
- **when** the event is (date and time)
- **where** the event is

Fill in the invitation below. Here is the information you will need:

Gator is having a swim party. It is for Tiger, who won a big swim meet. The party is on Saturday, June 3 at 2:00 p.m. It will be at the Critterville Community Pool.

Come to the party!

What: _____

For: _____

Date: _____

Time: _____

Place: _____

Just Practicing: Writing an Invitation

Create your own invitation below.

Don't forget to give all the information:

- Tell **what** the event is.
- Tell **who** the event is for.
- Tell **when** the event is. Include both the date and time.
- Tell **where** the event is.

After you write your invitation, decorate the border.

Addressing an Envelope

Letters, invitations, and notes are often mailed. To mail them, you will need to use an envelope. There is a special way to address an envelope.

Your Name
Your Street Address
Your City, State Zip Code

Person's Name
Person's Street Address
Person's City, State Zip Code

Here is an example:

Zachary Green
25 Little Lane
Dover, DE 02020

Shannon Brown
400 Main Street
Columbus, Ohio 55555

Just Practicing: Addressing an Envelope

Here are two envelopes for you to practice addressing. Address the envelopes to anyone you want! Look back at page 122 if you need help.

Writing Postcards

A **postcard** is a small card that can be sent in the mail. People write short notes on postcards. People often send postcards when they are on a trip. Postcards are mailed without envelopes. You can write the address and message, and then place a stamp right on the postcard.

Here is a postcard that Little Critter wrote to his friend Tiger.

July 7, 2002

Dear Tiger,

    I am having a cool time this summer. My family went to Critter World. I went on the Spider three times. I wish we could go on it together — just you and me!

              Your friend,
              Little Critter

Tiger
23 North Street
Critterville, U.S.A.

The other side of the postcard looks like this:

Just Practicing: Writing Postcards

Here are some blank postcards for you to write. Don't forget that the message goes on the left side, and the address goes on the right side.

message   address

Capitalization

 Remember: Use capital letters for the **names** of

people (or critters)	Gabby	Little Critter	Mr. Rubble
places	Critterville	Snow Hill	Main Street
months	January	April	September
days of the week	Monday	Wednesday	Friday
holidays	Thanksgiving	Fourth of July	Mother's Day

Circle the words below that need a capital letter. Then write each sentence correctly.

On saturday my friend, gabby, came over.

On Saturday my friend,
Gabby, came over.

We made our costumes for the (thanksgiving) play.

We made our costumes for
the Thanksgiving play.

I love (november) in (critterville.)

I love November in
Critterville.

Capitalization

 Remember: Capitalize the first word in a sentence.

We want to eat ice cream.

 Capitalize the main words in a book, movie, or song title.

I am reading a book called
How to Find Buried Treasure.

Circle the words below that need a capital letter. Then write each sentence correctly.

(the) class sang (happy birthday) to Tiger.

The class sang Happy
Birthday to Tiger.

(we) saw the movie, (just a scary monster,) on Friday.

We saw the movie, Just a
Scary Monster, on Friday.

(did) Gabby read (the mystery of the missing clue)?

Did Gabby read The
Mystery of the Missing Clue?

End Punctuation

 Remember:

★ Use a period (.) to end a sentence that makes a statement.

Gator met Little Critter at the bus stop.

★ Use a question mark (?) to end a sentence that asks a question.

Will they ride the bus today?

★ Use an exclamation point (!) to end a sentence that shows surprise or excitement.

Watch out!

Little Sister thinks she can put the right punctuation at the end of each sentence. Can you help her? Sure, you can!

Where is Tiger's baseball glove _?_

Malcolm has it _._

Oh, no _!_

What did Gabby do _?_

She found Malcolm's baseball glove _._

Cool _!_

Commas in Dates and Places

 Remember: Use commas in dates.

January 23, 2000
December 31, 1999
July 4, 1776

Use commas between the city and state when writing places.

Denver, Colorado
Columbus, Ohio
Albany, New York

Here are some dates and places. Can you put commas where they belong? The first one is done for you.

April 8, 1975   October 16, 1937   February 14, 2001

Austin, Texas   Miami, Florida   Boston, Massachusetts

Write your birthday on the line below. Put the comma where it belongs.

Answers will vary.

Write your address on the lines below. On the first line, write your street address. On the second line, write your city and state. Don't forget to use a comma!

Answers will vary.

Commas in a List

Remember: Use commas for words in a list.

Mom found cookies, marbles, and cars under my pillow.

Add commas to the sentences below. The first one is done for you.

There were clothes, games, and toys in my drawers.

The toy box was full of boats, trucks, and pajamas.

My sled, basketball, **and snorkel** were in the closet.

I keep pebbles, crayons, and money in my pocket.

All my robots, balls, and stuffed animals fit under my bed — almost.

Sentences

Remember: A sentence has a **beginning** and an **end**. A sentence tells a complete thought.

These are complete thoughts, so they are sentences:

Maurice and Molly are twins.
They like to have fun.

This is not a sentence because it does not tell a complete thought:

Maurice and Molly

Put these beginnings and endings together to make sentences. Mix them any way you want! Write the sentences on the lines below.

Gator   found a quarter.
After school, Gabby   missed the bus.
Malcolm   won at checkers.
        Suggested answers given.

Gator won at checkers

After school, Gabby missed the school bus.

Malcolm found a quarter.

Complete Thoughts: Endings

The sentences below have beginnings, but no endings. Can you finish each sentence so it tells a complete thought? The first one is done for you.

I get so mad when

I lose my pencil.

My best friend and I

        Answers will vary.

My favorite time of the year is

My pet likes to

Someday, I will

Complete Thoughts: Beginnings

The sentences below have endings, but no beginnings. Can you finish each sentence so it tells a complete thought? The first one is done for you.

Noises in the dark

        make me really scared.

        Answers will vary.

        yesterday.

        on my street.

        just for Grandma.

        in the summer.

Writing Sentences

Remember: A sentence tells a complete thought.

Little Sister loves to play hopscotch.

Write a sentence about each picture below. Be sure to have a beginning and an ending. Start each sentence with a capital letter and end it with a period.

_____
Answers will vary.
_____

_____
_____

_____
_____

Sentences in Order

Remember: The words in a sentence have a special order.

jumps high Grasshopper very

Grasshopper jumps very high.

Put the words in the right order. Be sure each sentence states a complete thought. Begin each sentence with a capital letter and end it with a period.

for toast breakfast eats Malcolm

Malcolm eats toast for breakfast.

a Birds eggs lay nest in

Birds lay eggs in a nest.

has balloon Little Sister a yellow

Little Sister has a yellow balloon.

Writing Statements

Remember: A sentence that tells you something is called a **statement**. This kind of sentence ends with a **period**.

My dog likes to dig.

My dog likes to dig.

Write a statement about each picture below. Begin each sentence with a capital letter and end it with a period.

_____
Answers will vary.
_____

_____
_____

_____
_____

_____
_____

_____
_____

Just Practicing: All About Me

Little Critter wants to know more about you. Read each question. Then answer each question with a sentence. Don't forget to begin each sentence with a capital letter and end it with a period.

What is your name? (Write **My Name is . . .**) Be sure to write your first, middle, and last names.

_____
Answers will vary.
_____

Where do you go to school?

_____
_____

What is your favorite holiday?

_____
_____

When is your birthday?

_____
_____

Writing Questions

Remember: A sentence that asks something is called a **question**. This kind of sentence ends with a **question mark**.

Do you want to play checkers?

Some words that begin a question are: **who, what, when,** and **where**.

Write a question about each picture below. Begin each question with a capital letter and end it with a question mark.

When is your party?

_____ Answers will vary. _____

Writing Exclamations

Remember: An **exclamation** is a sentence that shows excitement or emotion. This kind of sentence ends with an exclamation point.

Cool! Chocolate ice cream!

Oh, no! My dog ate my homework.

Write an exclamation about each picture below. Begin each sentence with a capital letter and end it with an exclamation point.

_____ Answers will vary. _____

Just Practicing: Statements

Write a statement about each of the things in Mr. Rubble's junkyard.

bird cage   radio   chair   television   tire

_____ Answers will vary. _____

Just Practicing: Questions

Little Critter is writing a story about Grandma's prize-winning berry pie. The story will be in the <u>Critterville News</u>. Can you write five questions he can ask Grandma about her pie?

_____ Answers will vary. _____

Just Practicing: Exclamations

Little Critter and his friends are at Tiger's surprise party. Can you write five things they might say that are exclamations? You can? Great!

_____
Answers will vary.
_____
_____
_____
_____
_____
_____
_____

The Five Senses

Can you name the five senses? Your senses help you understand the world around you. Match the pictures of the senses to the correct words.

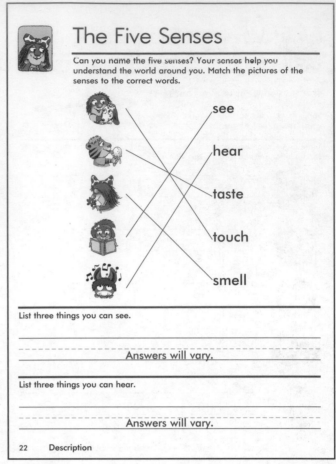

see

hear

taste

touch

smell

List three things you can see.

_____
_____
Answers will vary.

List three things you can hear.

_____
_____
Answers will vary.

Using the Five Senses to Describe

We can write special words to help us describe what we **see, hear, taste, touch,** and **smell**. Draw a line from each describing word to the picture that shows which sense is being used.

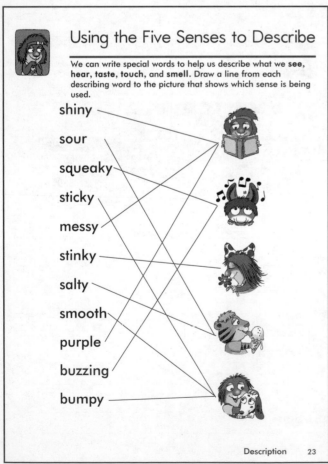

shiny

sour

squeaky

sticky

messy

stinky

salty

smooth

purple

buzzing

bumpy

Using Adjectives

Adjectives are describing words that tell us more about something. They make our writing more interesting.

what kind:	blue ribbon	old tire	little house
how many:	three kites	several trees	
how much:	lots of cookies	many bugs	
which one:	that book	those apples	this letter

Little Critter and Su Su both have dogs. Complete each sentence below by writing a describing word (**adjective**) in the blank. Use the word list to help you.

Word List				
funny	smart	yellow	curly	plain
pretty	playful	clean	small	fancy

Suggested answers given.

Little Critter's dog is ___playful___.

Su Su's dog is ___curly___.

Su Su is wearing two ___pretty___ bows.

Little Critter is wearing a ___yellow___ shirt.

Using Adjectives

Remember: **Adjectives** are describing words that tell **what kind, how many or how much,** and **which one.**

Look at each picture and write a word that describes it.

Answers will vary.

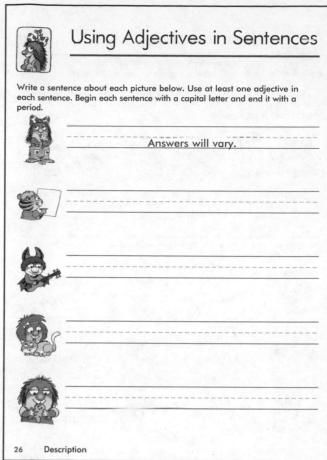

Using Adjectives in Sentences

Write a sentence about each picture below. Use at least one adjective in each sentence. Begin each sentence with a capital letter and end it with a period.

Answers will vary.

Using Adverbs

Adverbs are describing words that tell:

when:	yesterday	soon	now
where:	here	nearby	up
how:	quickly	carefully	happily
to what extent:	very	too	never

Little Critter's friends are having fun, running a race. Complete each sentence below by using a describing word (**adverb**) in the blank. Use the word list to help you.

Word List				
slowly	far	today	fast	up
too	very	well	down	soon

Suggested answers given.

Gabby can run **fast**.

The race will be over **soon**.

Malcolm ran **far**.

He fell **down**.

Little Critter is helping him get **up**.

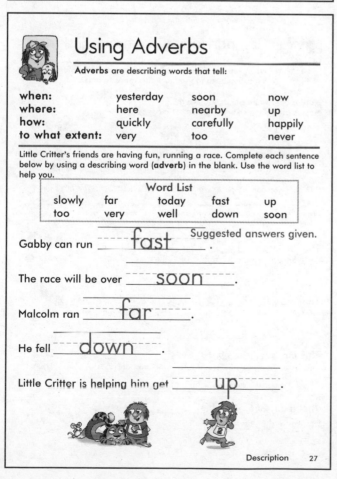

Using Adverbs in Sentences

Remember: **Adverbs** are describing words that tell **when, where, how,** and **to what extent.**

Write a sentence about each picture below. Use at least one adverb in each sentence. Begin each sentence with a capital letter and end it with a period. Here are some adverbs to help you, or you can think of your own.

Word List				
just	more	really	several	first
finally	then	fast	here	well

Answers will vary.

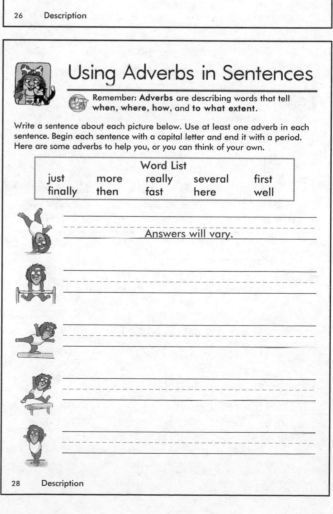

Description 25

26 Description

Description 27

28 Description

131

Using Verbs

 Remember: A **verb** is an **action** word.

walk   sing   talk   play

The verb in a sentence tells what is happening. You can use verbs to make your writing clearer and more interesting. Look at how a different verb is used in each sentence below.

Little Sister talked to Bun Bun.   **Little Sister** shouted at Bun Bun.   **Little Sister** whispered to Bun Bun.

Here are pairs of verbs. Circle the verb in each pair that describes the action more clearly.

 walks
(hikes)

 (jumps)
plays

 (builds)
makes

 sees
(finds)

 gets
(wins)

 takes
(grabs)

Description   29

Using Verbs in Sentences

Write your own sentences below. Choose the word from each pair that describes the action more clearly.

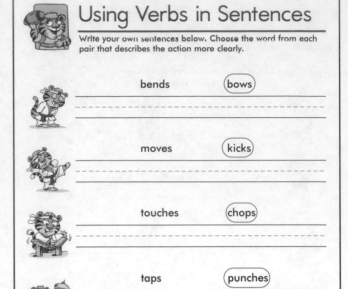

bends   (bows)

_____

moves   (kicks)

_____

touches   (chops)

_____

taps   (punches)

_____

(shouts)   says

_____

30   Description

Comparisons with **-er** and **-est**

 Sometimes you may need to describe something by comparing it to another thing. In this case, you may use the endings **-er** and **-est**.

The ending **-er** is used when comparing two things.
The ending **-est** is used when comparing three or more things.

Dad is tall.   Dad is taller.   Dad is the tallest.

Write the correct describing word on each line below.

Malcolm is ___**stronger**___.
strong   stronger   the strongest

Grasshopper is **the smallest**.
small   smaller   the smallest

Gator swims **faster**.
fast   faster   the fastest

Bun Bun jumps **high**.
high   higher   the highest

Description   31

Comparisons with **more** and **most**

 When you use a big word to compare one thing to another thing, you need to use the words **more** or **most**.

More is used when comparing two things.
Most is used when comparing three or more things.

This gift is wonderful.   This gift is more wonderful.   This gift is the most wonderful.

Write the correct describing word on each line below.

That picture is **more colorful**.
colorful   more colorful   the most colorful

That maze is **difficult**.
difficult   more difficult   the most difficult

This pie is **the most delicious**.
delicious   more delicious   the most delicious

That teddy bear is **more expensive**.
expensive   more expensive   the most expensive

32   Description

Comparisons with **like** or **as**

Another way to compare two things is to use **like** or **as**.

She sings. Birds sing.
So you can write:

> She sings like a bird.

The cookie is sweet. Honey is sweet.
So you can write:

> The cookie is as sweet as honey.

Complete the sentences using clues from the pictures and the words below.

bunny	hungry	soft
teakettle	horse	baby

Her coat is as **soft** as a **bunny**.

Little Critter whistled like a **teakettle**.

Tiger is as **hungry** as a **horse**.

Little Sister cried like a **baby**.

Comparisons with **like** or **as**

Comparisons with like or as

Use the word list to fill in the blanks in these comparisons. Write the sentences on the lines below.

Word List			
twinkle	swim	pillow	sticky
soft	stars	tape	fish

I can _____ like a _____.

I can swim like a fish.

The floor is as _____ as _____.

The floor is as sticky as tape.

Her eyes _____ like _____.

Her eyes twinkle like stars.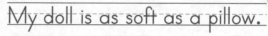

My doll is as _____ as a _____.

My doll is as soft as a pillow.

Writing Descriptive Sentences

Look around at all the fun that's going on. Can you write five descriptive sentences about what you see? Be sure to begin each sentence with a capital letter and end it with a period. Use describing words, comparisons, and verbs to make your sentences interesting.

Answers will vary.

Describing People

You can use lots of describing words when you write about people. Think about how the person **looks**. Describe the person's (or critter's) size, hair, and clothes.

Bat Child is short.
He has big, brown wings.
His ears stand straight up.
He wears a yellow shirt and purple pants.

Look at the describing words above. Can you think of more describing words for the critters below? Write at least three describing words (for each critter) on the lines below.

Answers will vary.

Describing People

Here are some words you can use when describing a person, his or her clothes, and his or her hair.

Draw a person in the box below. Then write four sentences that describe the person. You may use the word list to help you.

Pictures will vary.

Word List

tall	curly	large
round	fuzzy	small
thin	straight	striped
short	dark	dotted
medium	light	plain
strong	long	silly

Answers will vary.

Writing Riddles

A fun way to practice using words that describe is to write a **riddle**. A riddle is a puzzle. You must read the description and then try to guess what the thing is that is being described. Here is an example:

I keep things safe.
I have a hole in my middle.
A key will open me.
Can you guess what I am?

I am a lock.

Read each of the riddles below and guess what is being described.

I know the numbers 1 through 12.
I have two hands.
My hands move all day long.
Can you guess what I am?

I am a ___clock___.

My name is the same as what I do.
People try to swat at me.
Can you guess what I am?

I am a ___fly___.

I lay around all the time.
Everyone steps on me, but it doesn't hurt.
Dogs like to sleep on me.
Can you guess what I am?

I am a ___rug___.

Writing Riddles

You can write riddles, too! Look at the pictures below. Write a riddle for each object, using the describing words in the box. Or, you can use your own describing words.

Riddles will vary.

round
metal
president
save
bank

I am a coin.

Riddles will vary.

numbers
straight
inches
measure
wood
plastic

I am a ruler.

Writing More Riddles

Keep practicing! Making up riddles will help you use interesting words in all your writing!

Riddles will vary.

tail
wind
paper
string
fly

I am a kite.

Riddles will vary.

hot
wood
cook
glow
bright
camp

I am a fire.

Just Practicing: My Family and Me

Draw a picture of your family in the box below. Then use describing words to tell all about you and your family.

Pictures will vary.

My Family and Me

Answers will vary.

Just Practicing: All About My Stuff

Draw a picture of your favorite stuff: toys, books, sports things — whatever you like to play with or collect. Then use describing words to tell all about your stuff.

Pictures will vary.

All About My Stuff

Answers will vary.

The Writing Process

The Writing Process is a set of steps to help you make your writing the best it can be. Read about the Writing Process below. You'll get to try each step on your own in the pages that follow.

1 ### Prewriting
Prewriting is what you do before you write. It is a way of collecting your thoughts and ideas for what you want to write about. Sometimes it is called **brainstorming**.

2 ### Drafting
Your first try at a piece of writing is called a **rough draft**. When you write a rough draft, don't worry about spelling and punctuation — just get your writing started!

3 ### Revising
Revising means making corrections. When you revise your writing, you want to be sure it makes sense. You want to make sure nothing is missing. This is also a good time to check that you have used interesting words.

4 ### Proofreading
When you **proofread** your writing, you are looking for mistakes. Now, it is time to check your spelling, punctuation, and to make sure you capitalized words correctly.

5 ### Publishing
When you **publish** your writing, you are ready for people to read it! You should use your best handwriting and a nice clean piece of paper. Or, you can type what you have written on a computer.

Prewriting

The first step of the writing process is called prewriting. **Pre-** means **before**, so **prewriting** means **before writing**.

This is the time when you get to think about writing. Here are some questions you can ask yourself when you are prewriting:

- What do I want to write about?
- What do I know a lot about?
- Where can I find information?
- What are some words or ideas I can use for my topic?

Now let's practice doing some prewriting!

One fun topic to write about is ANIMALS. Can you answer these prewriting questions about ANIMALS? Write down whatever you think of.

What animals do I want to write about?

Answers will vary.

What animal do I know a lot about?

What are some words or ideas about that animal?

Where can I find more information about that animal?

Prewriting — Brainstorming

One way to **prewrite** is to **brainstorm**.

Brainstorming means thinking of everything you can think of about a topic. Then you write down each idea.

You will make a list of words and ideas about your topic. There are no right or wrong words, or good or bad ideas. Just write whatever comes into your brain.

Here's a topic to brainstorm. Little Critter has started a list. Can you add lots of your own words and ideas?

A Day at the Beach

sand	playing	big waves
water	finding stuff	
	Answers will vary.	

Prewriting — Writing Webs

Another prewriting method is **writing webs**, also called story webs or clustering. Again, you think of everything you can about a topic. Then you write each idea down like this:

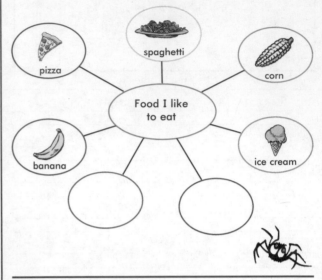

pizza

spaghetti

corn

Food I like to eat

banana

ice cream

Can you add two more ideas to this web?

Answers will vary.

Prewriting — Writing Webs

Here is a topic for you. Can you fill in the web with words and ideas that you could write about?

Answers will vary.

Things my friends and I like to do

Prewriting — Freewriting

Another kind of prewriting is called **freewriting**. It is just what it sounds like. You are **free** to **write** whatever comes to mind.

You just start writing and keep going. Don't worry about what fits. Don't worry about spelling or capitals or punctuation. You can fix all that later.

Freewriting helps your ideas come out! Just write . . . and write . . . and write!

Little Critter did some freewriting. Read what he wrote, and then answer the question below.

> I like animals. I have a goldfish. Mom says I am responsible for her. She lives in a goldfish bowl. She likes to swim. I like to swim, too. Sometimes I forget to feed her. But Mom reminds me.

Can you figure out what Little Critter's topic was?

Little Critter's pet

Just Practicing: Brainstorming

Here are some topics that Gabby and Little Critter like to write about. Pick one topic and do your own **brainstorming** below.

My Vacation
Just Me and My Dog
Going to the Fair
When I Grow Up
A Job I Did

Title: _____

Answers will vary.

Just Practicing: Writing Webs

Now it's time for you to make your own writing web. First, choose your topic. What kinds of things do you know a lot about? Gator has some ideas to get you started.

| dinosaurs | planets | magic tricks |
| on the farm | car games | places to go |

Answers will vary.

Just Practicing: Freewriting

Now it's time for you to do your own freewriting. Choose a topic from the pictures you see. Then write, write, write — whatever you think of about that topic.

Answers will vary.

Just Practicing: Prewriting Your Way

Which kind of prewriting do you like best?

brainstorming   writing webs   freewriting

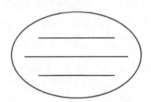

Use whichever kind of prewriting you want as you prewrite about:

My Very Best Day at School

Answers will vary.

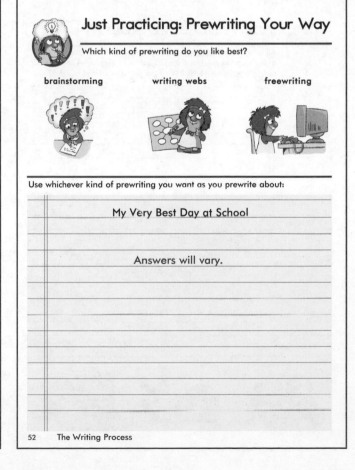

Drafting

Step two of the writing process is called **drafting**. It is time to take all of the ideas and words you came up with during prewriting and begin to write the real thing.

Let's practice using this topic: **Going to the Farm**.

Start by doing some prewriting. What do you see in the pictures? What do you know about going to a farm?

Answers will vary.

Drafting

Now it's time to write a draft. Look at all of the ideas you have about **Going to the Farm**. Which ones go together? Take the ideas and words and make complete sentences.

Example: cows, chickens, horses, goats

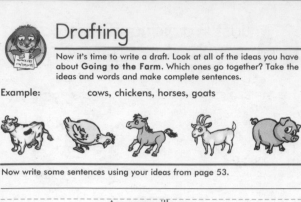

Now write some sentences using your ideas from page 53.

Answers will vary.

Just Practicing: Rough Draft

All of the sentences you **drafted** on page 54 can be put in order to make a story. Can you put your sentences together so your story makes sense? Try it on the lines below.

Answers will vary.

Revising

After drafting, it is time for step three of the writing process: **revising**. To revise means **to change**.

Look closely at what you have written. You can ask yourself questions such as:

- Does this make sense?
- Have I used interesting words?
- Am I missing anything?
- Does everything belong here?
- Should I take something out?
- Do I have things in a good order?

Revise the sentences until you have a better story. Don't worry about spelling, punctuation, or capitals yet. That will come next.

Look at the sentences below. Revise each one to make it a more interesting sentence. Then draw a line to the number to show which sentence should come first, second, and third.

After school, I did something.

Answers will vary.

That night, I read something.

Before school, I ate something.

1

2

3

Attention writers! Sometimes you will revise more than once before a sentence or story is really terrific.

Just Practicing: Revising

Remember: When you **revise**, ask yourself these questions:

- Does this make sense?
- Have I used interesting words?
- Am I missing anything?
- Does everything belong here?
- Should I take something out?
- Do I have things in a good order?

Look at the story you wrote on page 55. Revise it on the lines below.

Answers will vary.

How does your story look now? Is it better?
Show your story to a parent or teacher. Does he or she have any ideas to help you revise it even more?

Proofreading

Is your story better now? If you need to revise it more, use another piece of paper.

When you are finished revising, it is time for step four of the writing process: **proofreading**.

Now you can fix mistakes in

- spelling
- punctuation
- capitalization

Here are some proofreading marks that will help you. See how they are used in the story below.

Proofreading Marks
- ⬭ misspelling
- ≡ make a capital letter
- ⊙ add a period
- ? add a question mark

I went to (schoool) yesterday. I forgot my books⊙They were at home. Why did I forget them? My dog, blue, was sleeping on (then) miss kitty didn't scold me. She was really nice to (mee) Maybe Miss Kitty has a dog at her house, (to.)

Proofreading

It is time to practice **proofreading**.
Remember: You are looking for mistakes in:

- **spelling**   I caught (for) fish.
- **punctuation**   Wait! You can't go there⊙
- **capitalization** miss kitty has a dog at home.

Proofreading Marks
- ⬭ misspelling
- ≡ make a capital letter
- ⊙ add a period
- ! add an exclamation point
- ? add a question mark

The proofreading marks are here to help you.

Proofread the following sentences.

It's lunch time! We have fun (eeting) our lunch with Bat child. he does (magick) tricks for us⊙Wow! Look at how he makes my spoon disappear! Can he make it come back? I sure hope so. I want to eat my pudding.

Proofread these sentences, too.

The critterville team has a game on (tusday.)

Who are they playing? We want (too) go watch (tham)

Let's go, together. Meet me at (twelve) o'clock.

Just Practicing: Proofreading

The more you practice **proofreading**, the better your writing will be.

Proofreading Marks
- ⬭ misspelling
- ≡ make a capital letter
- ⊙ add a period
- ! add an exclamation point
- ? add a question mark

Practice by proofreading the sentences below. Write the corrected sentences on the lines.

I slept in a tent (wen) we went camping ⊙

I slept in a tent when we went camping.

Did you see me (mak) a home run ?

Did you see me make a home run?

My (freinds) and I had fun in our clubhouse ⊙

My friends and I had fun in our clubhouse.

There was a (pudle) next to my dog ⊙

There was a puddle next to my dog.

Will you read me a (storie) about super critter ?

Will you read me a story about Super Critter?

Publishing

Remember: Step five of the writing process is called **publishing**.

There are lots of ways to publish your writing. Look at the examples below.

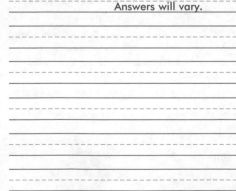

How would you publish your writing?

Proofreading and Publishing

Now go back to your story on page 57. Read what you wrote. Proofread your story for mistakes.

Now write the **final draft** on the lines below.

Answers will vary.

Step five of the writing process is called publishing.

It happens when your writing is finished. You have fixed the mistakes. You have written or typed your story neatly. Now it is ready for others to read.

Show your story to a friend, to a parent, or to a teacher. When you have done all of these things, you have published your writing!

My Summer Vacation

Remember: The writing process is made of these steps:

Step One
Prewriting

Step Two
Drafting

Step Three
Revising

Step Four
Proofreading

Step Five
Publishing

You can use the following pages to write a story about your summer vacation — a real one or an imaginary one. Start on this page. You can do brainstorming or a writing web or freewriting. Put your prewriting here.

My Summer Vacation

Answers will vary.

My Summer Vacation

Use your prewriting to go to the next step: **drafting**. Use your ideas to write complete sentences. This is your draft.

My Summer Vacation

Answers will vary.

My Summer Vacation

Read your first draft. How can you make it better? It is time to go to the next step: **revising.** If you need to, go back to page 56 and look at the questions you can ask yourself as you revise. Write your new draft below.

My Summer Vacation

Answers will vary.

Now, read your draft. It is time for proofreading. Use the proofreading marks to fix the mistakes.
Then write your story without the mistakes on the next page. Be sure to let someone read it!

My Summer Vacation

My Summer Vacation
by

(your name)

Answers will vary.

The Main Idea

The **main idea** tells what a story is mostly about. Every story has a main idea.

Here is an example:

Little Critter gets a haircut.

Look at the pictures below. Put a check mark (✓) in front of the best main idea for each picture.

_____ Sports are fun.
✓ Three friends have a contest.
_____ Gabby can jump.

_____ Dogs make good pets.
_____ The dog is ready to play.
✓ Dogs like to bury things.

The Main Idea

Remember: The **main idea** tells what a picture or story is mostly about.

Write the main idea for each picture below. Be sure to write a complete sentence. Start with a capital letter and end with a period.

Suggested answers given.

 Little Critter is feeding his dog.

 Dad is fishing.

 Tiger is playing soccer.

Writing a Title

The name of a picture or story is called a **title**. The title tells the main idea.

Here is an example:

Super Critter to the Rescue

Look at the pictures below. Put a check mark (✓) in front of the best title for each picture.

_____ Little Sister Loves Summer

✓ Little Sister Plays in the Pool

_____ Little Sister Wants Summer to Come

_____ Grandpa Has a New Hat

_____ Grandpa Wants to Fish

✓ Grandpa Goes Fishing

Writing a Title

Remember: The **title** is the name of the story or picture.

Write a title for each picture below. Be sure to use capital letters for the important words.

Suggested answers given.

 Little Critter and his sister play basketball.

 The Critters have fun at Critterland.

 Little Critter takes a bath.

Story Parts

Every story has a **beginning**, a **middle**, and an **end**.

beginning
Gator collected rocks.

middle
He sorted the rocks.

end
He made a display.

Draw lines to show which picture is the beginning, which is the middle, and which is the end.

beginning

middle

end

beginning

middle

end

Story Parts

Remember: Every story has a **beginning**, a **middle**, and an **end**.

Can you fill in the beginning, middle, and end of this story? Write sentences to complete the story.

Planting Vegetables

Beginning

Answers will vary.

Middle

Answers will vary.

End

Answers will vary.

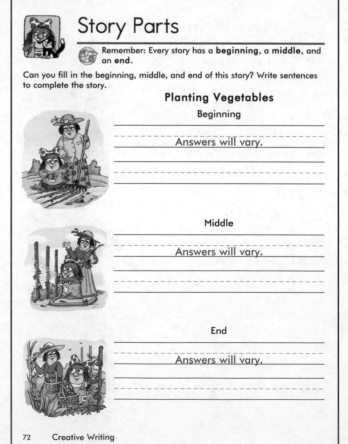

Setting — Place

Every story has a setting. The **setting** is the **place** where the story happens.

You will need to describe the setting so your reader can "see" it.

Here is an example:

    Dad and I went camping. Our <u>campsite</u> was really <u>cool</u>. We were <u>surrounded by lots of big, leafy trees</u>. We pitched our tent <u>near a huge rock</u>. The <u>lake was so close</u> we could <u>see it from our tent</u>. We used <u>branches and twigs on the ground for our campfire</u>. That night <u>it was so dark</u>, I could <u>see a zillion stars in the sky</u>. It was <u>great out there</u> — just the campfire, my dad, and me!

Can you "see" the place that Little Critter is telling about? Underline all of the words that describe the setting.

Creative Writing   73

Setting — Time

The setting is the place where the story happens. But the **setting** is also the **time** in which the story happens.

Your reader needs to know when the story is happening.

Look again at this example:

    Dad and I went camping. Our campsite was really cool. We were surrounded by lots of big, leafy trees. We pitched our tent near a huge rock. The lake was so close we could see it from our tent. We used branches and twigs on the ground for our campfire. <u>That night</u> it was so dark, I could see a zillion stars in the sky. It was great out there — just the campfire, my dad, and me!

Can you find the words that describe the time of day? Underline all of the words that describe the time this story is about.

74   Creative Writing

Just Practicing: Setting — Place

 Remember: The **setting** includes the **place** where the story happens.

Think of a place that you know well. It could be a room, your neighborhood, a special place you visited, or an imaginary place.

Brainstorm some words and ideas about that place. Think about what you **see, hear, smell, taste,** or **feel** in that place.

Place: _____

Answers will vary.

Creative Writing   75

Just Practicing: Setting — Time

Now add the other part of **setting: time.**

Go back to page 75. Add sentences that describe the time. Time can be

* time of day
* a holiday
* season of the year
* a time in history
* a time in the future

It answers the question: When is this story happening?

Read the following story. Then answer the questions below.

    It was getting dark. The wind blew against my face. I felt snowflakes hit my nose. I put my hood up over my head. I looked up at a clock in a store window. In fifteen minutes, it would be suppertime.

What time of day is it?

It is evening.

What season of the year is it?

It is winter.

What is the weather like?

It is snowing.

76   Creative Writing

Just Practicing:
Setting — Place and Time

Gator wants to write a story about what happened when he went rock collecting in the desert. What are some words he can use to describe the setting?

Place	Time
Answers will vary.	

Just Practicing:
Setting — Place and Time

Gabby wants to write a story about what happened on Snow Hill last weekend. What are some words she can use to describe the setting?

Place	Time
Answers will vary.	

My Room

Little Critter wants to know what your room looks like. Can you write some sentences that describe what it is like to be in your room?

Think of describing words. What do you **see**, **hear**, **smell**, **taste**, or **feel** when you are in your room?

 Prewriting space: Brainstorming, writing a web, or freewriting? You choose!

Answers will vary.

My Room

Look at the describing words you wrote on page 79. Now write sentences using some of the words.
Write your draft below.

Answers will vary.

Characters

The people (or animals or critters) the story is about are the **characters.** Every story has at least one character. The character may even be you!

The reader of the story needs to "see" the characters. It is important to describe each one. There are lots of things to tell about when describing a character:

age	young	grown-up	teenager
size	short	skinny	large
clothes	neat	comfortable	messy
features (hair, eyes, mouth, etc.)	curly	dark	smiling
personality	kind	silly	shy
mood	nervous	tired	happy

Look at the picture below and write three words to describe the character.

Answers will vary.

Characters

Remember: A **character** is someone who the story is about. Can you write three words to describe each character below?

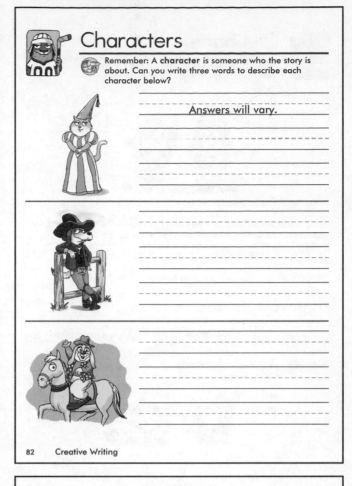

Answers will vary.

Characters

What if you were the **character** in your story? Can you describe yourself? Start by drawing a picture of yourself.

Pictures will vary.

Now write some sentences that describe YOU.

Answers will vary.

Characters and Setting

Read the story below. Underline all of the words that describe the **character.** Then circle all of the words that describe the **setting.**

A Day at the Playground

Blue and I had all day to play. Blue is my spotted dog. We went to the playground near the school. I wore my old, blue overalls and my striped shirt. Blue wore his red collar. The playground was empty. We could play on the big slide without waiting in line. Blue dug a few holes in the sand. Then we raced to the new yellow bench and back again. We had fun!

Dialogue

When characters talk, the words they say are called **dialogue**. Writing dialogue is easy, but you need to use special punctuation.

"Let's go to the clubhouse," said Gabby.

Little Critter answered, "Okay with me!"

The words a character speaks are put in quotation marks ("").

You separate the dialogue ("Let's go to the clubhouse") from the information about who is speaking (said Gabby) with a comma (,).

Put in the correct punctuation in the sentences below. The first one has been done for you.

"Here's some jelly for our sandwiches," said Molly.

Maurice said, "I'll get the peanut butter."

Mom told Dad, "Little Sister needs new shoes."

"We can go shopping tomorrow," he answered.

Dialogue

Remember: The words characters say are called **dialogue**.

Sometimes dialogue is a question and uses a question mark (?).

"Who is ready for dessert?" asked Mom.

Mom asked, "Who is ready for dessert?"

And sometimes dialogue is an exclamation and uses an exclamation point (!).

"Watch out!" cried Tiger.

Tiger cried, "Watch out!"

Put in the correct punctuation in the sentences below.

"Where is my glove?" asked Tiger.

"Did you lose it?" asked Gator.

Little Critter asked, "Do you want to play?"

Gabby yelled, "Be careful!"

"Thanks!" Maurice and Molly yelled back.

Writing Dialogue

Now you can write some **dialogue**. Think of what you want Dad and Little Critter to say to each other. Then fill in the dialogue on the lines below.

"_____ Answers will vary. _____,"

said Dad.

"_____ Answers will vary. _____,"

said Little Critter.

"_____ Answers will vary. _____,"

said Dad.

Just Practicing: Writing Dialogue

What are these characters saying to each other? Write the dialogue below.

Answers will vary.

Answers will vary.

The Problem

An interesting story usually has a **problem** that needs to be solved. Describe the problem in the pictures below.

Problem:

Malcolm is going too fast.

Problem:

Answers will vary.

Problem:

Answers will vary.

The Solution

Now that we have a problem, we need to solve the problem. The answer to a problem is called a **solution**. Describe a way to solve each problem in the pictures below. Be creative! Use your imagination.

Solution:

Malcolm should slow down.

Solution:

Answers will vary.

Solution:

Answers will vary.

The Problem and the Solution

Now, make up your own problem and solution. Draw a picture of your problem and solution and describe them below.

Problem:

Answers will vary.

Solution:

Answers will vary.

Setting, Characters, and the Problem

Remember:

- The place and time in a story is the **setting**.
- The people a story is about are the **characters**.
- The problem in a story is the **conflict**.

Read the story below. Then answer the questions about setting, characters, and conflict on the next page.

After lunch, the sun was covered by lots of clouds. Little Sister and I knew it was going to rain. We sat by the window and watched the sky get darker and darker.

Soon rain was falling and the wind was blowing. Little Sister looked scared. She doesn't like storms. I told her it would be okay. Then we heard loud thunder. The lights went out. Little Sister crawled under the table. Soon she was fast asleep.

When she woke up, the storm was over. I am glad she didn't see all the lightning! It was scary!

Setting, Characters, and the Problem

Answer the following questions about the story on page 92.

Who are the characters in the story?

Little Critter and

Little Sister

What is the setting of the story? (time and place)

It is the afternoon.

at home by the window

What are some words used to describe the setting?

sky got darker

thunder and lightning

What is the problem in the story?

Little Sister doesn't like

storms.

Creative Writing   93

Picture Stories — Comics

Do you like to read comics? So does Little Critter! He reads them every day! Sometimes he likes to draw them, too.

Comics are stories, too. They use setting and characters — and there's usually a problem.   Suggested answers given.

Who are the **characters** in Little Critter's comic strip?

Critters

Super Critter

What is the **setting**?

a tiny island

a boat

What is the **problem**?

Critters stranded on an island.

94   Creative Writing

Picture Stories — Comics

Can you draw your own comic strip? Be sure to write what the characters are saying to each other. Think about the setting, characters, and a problem.

Who are the **characters** in your comic strip?

Answers will vary.

What is the **setting**?

Answers will vary.

What is the **problem**?

Answers will vary.

Creative Writing   95

Just Practicing: Comics

Here is another place for you to create a comic strip! Have fun!

Who are the **characters** in your comic strip?

Answers will vary.

What is the **setting**?

Answers will vary.

What is the **problem**?

Answers will vary.

96   Creative Writing

Just Practicing: Story Starters

Here is a story that Little Critter started to write. Finish the story on the lines below. Begin by describing the setting.

When I woke up, I looked out the window and saw . . .

_____ Answers will vary. _____

Just Practicing: Story Starters

Here is the beginning of another story. As you finish writing it, add some dialogue.

I was so mad when . . .

_____ Answers will vary. _____

Just Practicing: Story Starters

Finish the story that Gabby started below. Think of a problem to make the story interesting.

One day last summer, my dad and I went . . .

_____ Answers will vary. _____

Journal Writing

A **journal** is a special book for your own writing. It is a kind of diary.

There are no rules about writing in a journal. Here are some ideas to help you learn about journal writing.

- You can write every day or just when you want to.
- You can write whatever you want: stories, poems, "what I did today," or anything!
- No one has to read your journal but you.
- You can write, draw, or paste in stuff you want to keep.
- It helps if you put the date on the page when you write. Then you will know when you wrote that page.

Look at a page in Little Critter's journal. This is what he wrote last summer:

> July 4, 2001
>
> Today is the Fourth of July. We had a picnic in our backyard. Grandma and Grandpa came. Dad cooked stuff on the grill. Mom made fresh corn and fruit salad.
>
> But the best part was at night. We saw lots of fireworks! They were big and bright. And loud! Little Sister put her hands over her ears. But I didn't. I liked the loud noise. I laughed and laughed.

Just Practicing: Journal Writing

Write your own journal entry on the lines below. Write about anything you want. Be sure to put a date at the top of the entry.

Answers will vary.

Just Practicing: A Pirate's Journal

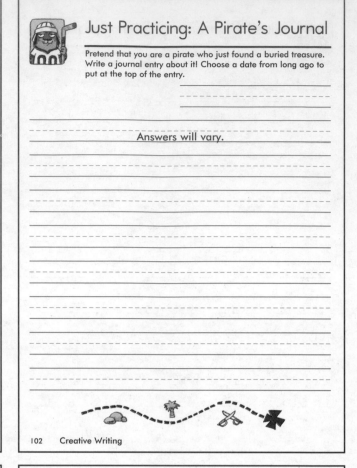

Pretend that you are a pirate who just found a buried treasure. Write a journal entry about it! Choose a date from long ago to put at the top of the entry.

Answers will vary.

Just Practicing: My Autobiography

An **autobiography** is the story of the life of the person who writes it.

Some things to include in your **autobiography** are:

- when you were born
- where you were born
- information about your family: their names, relationships, etc.
- places you have lived
- things you have done

Think about those things. Then use the space below to prewrite ideas you want to include in your autobiography. You can brainstorm, use writing webs, or freewrite.

Answers will vary.

Just Practicing: My Autobiography

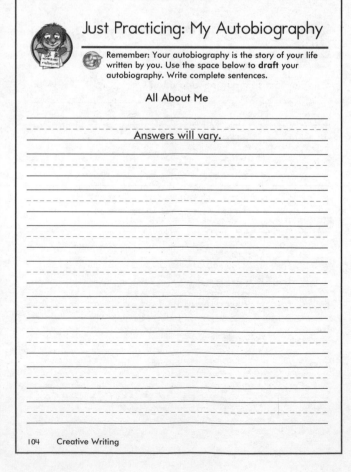

Remember: Your autobiography is the story of your life written by you. Use the space below to **draft** your autobiography. Write complete sentences.

All About Me

Answers will vary.

Just Practicing: My Autobiography

Use the space below to **revise** the draft of your autobiography. Ask yourself:

* Am I missing anything?
* Do I have everything in good order?
* Should I take anything out?
* Does everything belong here?
* Have I used interesting verbs and describing words?

All About Me

Answers will vary.

Just Practicing: My Autobiography

Go back to page 105 and **proofread** what you have written. Look for mistakes in spelling, capitalization, and punctuation. Then write your **final draft** below.

All About Me

Answers will vary.

To **publish** your autobiography, just let someone read all about you!

What Is a Paragraph?

A **paragraph** is a group of sentences that are about the same idea. Read the paragraph below.

(Little Critter knows how to take good care of his dog, Blue.) He gives Blue fresh food and water every day. He takes his dog out for walks so that Blue can get exercise. He brushes Blue's fur once a day and gives him a bath once a week. When Blue is not feeling well, Little Critter takes him to the vet. With such good care, Blue stays happy and healthy, and that makes Little Critter happy, too!

Look at the paragraph again. Circle the sentence that tells what the paragraph is mostly about.

Did you circle this sentence?

Little Critter knows how to take good care of his dog, Blue.

If you did, you are right! The first sentence in a paragraph usually tells what the paragraph is mostly about. This is called the **topic sentence.** The rest of the sentences in the paragraph tell about how Little Critter takes good care of his dog.

What Belongs and What Doesn't Belong

Remember: A **paragraph** is a group of sentences about the **same idea.**

Look at the paragraph below. Some of the sentences do not belong. They are underlined.

Little Critter knows how to take good care of his dog, Blue. He gives Blue fresh food and water every day. <u>One day, Little Critter forgot to turn off the water.</u> He takes his dog out for walks so that Blue can get exercise. He brushes Blue's fur once a day and gives him a bath once a week. <u>Mrs. Critter made a red sweater for Blue.</u> With such good care, Blue stays happy and healthy, and that makes Little Critter happy, too!

When you find a sentence that does not go with the paragraph topic sentence, you should take it out. Underline the sentences in the paragraph below that do not belong.

Making an ice cream cone is easy. First, get the ice cream from the freezer. <u>Mom bought some frozen juice, too!</u> Next, get a cone and an ice cream scoop. Now scoop out some ice cream from the container. <u>Chocolate is my favorite flavor.</u> Put the ice cream on the cone. You're all done!

Writing Paragraphs

Now, look at the paragraph on page 107 again.

Did you notice that the first sentence does not line up with the other sentences? It starts a little over to the right. That is called **indenting**. You should always **indent** the first sentence in a paragraph.

Finish writing the paragraph below. The **topic sentence** is written for you. Notice that it is **indented**!

Don't forget that the sentences you add must be about the **topic sentence**.

    I know how to help my mom and dad.

Answers will vary.

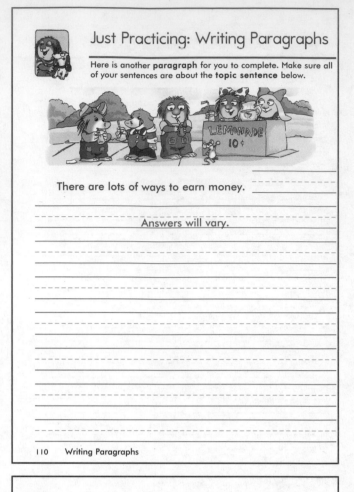

Just Practicing: Writing Paragraphs

Here is another **paragraph** for you to complete. Make sure all of your sentences are about the **topic sentence** below.

There are lots of ways to earn money.

Answers will vary.

Just Practicing: Writing Paragraphs

Now, write your own paragraph about the picture below. Remember:

- **Indent** the first sentence of your paragraph.
- Your first sentence is usually your **topic sentence**. It tells what the paragraph is mostly about.
- All the sentences that follow should be about your topic sentence.

Answers will vary.

Using Order Words

When you write a paragraph, you need to make the order of events clear. Using **order words** will help. Here are some order words you can use.

first	next	now	finally
second	then	later	last

Look at the pictures below. Label each picture in order. Use these words:

      first   **next**   **last**

next   first   last

Look at the pictures below. Label each picture in order. Use these words:

      first   **then**   **finally**

finally   first   then

Using Order Words

Remember: Using **order words** makes your writing clearer.

Read the paragraph below. Without order words, this paragraph is not clear. Write an order word in each of the blanks. Use the list on page 112 to help you.

Suggested answers given.

Bun Bun wants to send out birthday party invitations.

____First____ she will make a list of her friends.

____Then____ she will write her name on each invitation.

____Next____ she will write the date and time of the party. ____Then____ Bun Bun will address each envelope and put on a stamp. ____Finally____ she will go to the post office and put the invitations in the mailbox. The invitations are on their way!

Just Practicing: Using Order Words

Use **order words** when you write the following paragraph. Be sure to **indent** the first sentence.

How to Make Little Critter's Favorite Sandwich

Answers will vary.

Parts of a Friendly Letter

Friendly letters are fun to write. It's nice to send letters to friends and relatives. And it's great to get a letter, too. There are rules about writing letters. Every letter is made of these parts.

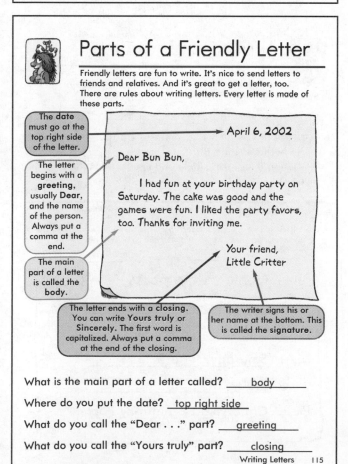

The **date** must go at the top right side of the letter.

The letter begins with a **greeting,** usually **Dear,** and the name of the person. Always put a comma at the end.

The main part of a letter is called the **body.**

The letter ends with a **closing.** You can write **Yours truly** or **Sincerely.** The first word is capitalized. Always put a comma at the end of the closing.

The writer signs his or her name at the bottom. This is called the **signature.**

April 6, 2002

Dear Bun Bun,

I had fun at your birthday party on Saturday. The cake was good and the games were fun. I liked the party favors, too. Thanks for inviting me.

Your friend,
Little Critter

What is the main part of a letter called? ____body____

Where do you put the date? __top right side__

What do you call the "Dear . . ." part? ____greeting____

What do you call the "Yours truly" part? ____closing____

Parts of a Friendly Letter

Can you label the parts of a friendly letter? Put these words where they go in the boxes below.

signature   greeting   date   closing   body

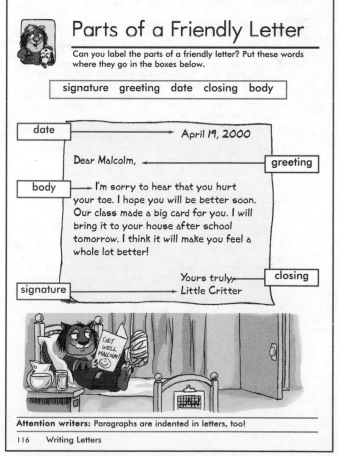

date → April 19, 2000

Dear Malcolm, ← greeting

body → I'm sorry to hear that you hurt your toe. I hope you will be better soon. Our class made a big card for you. I will bring it to your house after school tomorrow. I think it will make you feel a whole lot better!

Yours truly, ← closing
signature → Little Critter

Attention writers: Paragraphs are indented in letters, too!

Just Practicing: Writing a Friendly Letter

Mr. Rubble let Little Critter have a piece of junk from the junkyard. Now Little Critter wants to write him and tell him what he did with it.

Pretend you are Little Critter and write a letter to Mr. Rubble. Some parts of the letter are filled in to help you. (Hint: Look back at page 19 to see things in Mr. Rubble's Junkyard.)

_____
(date)

Dear _____,
(greeting)

I_____

_____
Answers will vary.

(body)

_____

_____

_____

_____

Sincerely,
(closing)

Little Critter
(signature)

Just Practicing: Writing a Friendly Letter

Tiger just won a karate match. He wants to write a letter to his cousin about the match.

Pretend you are Tiger and write a letter to your cousin. Make sure to use commas in the date, the greeting, and the closing. (Hint: Look at page 30 to see Tiger practicing karate.)

_____

_____

_____

Answers will vary.

_____

_____

_____

_____

_____

Just Practicing: Writing a Thank You Note

A **thank you note** is like a friendly letter. You include all of the same parts: **date, greeting, body, closing,** and **signature.** But it is special because it is written for one reason: to thank someone for something.

Gabby's aunt sent her a new book — The Haunted Cave Mystery. Gabby wants to thank her for it. Pretend you are Gabby and write a thank you note to your aunt. Look back at page 115 if you need help.

_____

_____

_____

Answers will vary.

_____

_____

_____

_____

_____

_____

Writing an Invitation

An **invitation** is a short note with one purpose: to ask someone to come to something, like a birthday party, wedding, or other celebration.

An invitation must give information about:

- **what** the event is
- **who** the event is for
- **when** the event is (date and time)
- **where** the event is

Fill in the invitation below. Here is the information you will need:

Gator is having a swim party. It is for Tiger, who won a big swim meet. The party is on Saturday, June 3 at 2:00 p.m. It will be at the Critterville Community Pool.

Come to the party!

What: swim party

For: Tiger

Date: Saturday, June 3

Time: 2:00 p.m.

Place: Critterville Community Pool

Just Practicing: Writing an Invitation

Create your own invitation below.

Don't forget to give all the information:

- Tell **what** the event is.
- Tell **who** the event is for.
- Tell **when** the event is. Include both the date and time.
- Tell **where** the event is.

After you write your invitation, decorate the border.

Addressing an Envelope

Letters, invitations, and notes are often mailed. To mail them, you will need to use an envelope. There is a special way to address an envelope.

Your Name
Your Street Address
Your City, State Zip Code

      Person's Name
      Person's Street Address
      Person's City, State Zip Code

Here is an example:

Zachary Green
25 Little Lane
Dover, DE 02020

      Shannon Brown
      400 Main Street
      Columbus, Ohio 55555

Just Practicing: Addressing an Envelope

Here are two envelopes for you to practice addressing. Address the envelopes to anyone you want! Look back at page 122 if you need help.

Answers will vary.

Writing Postcards

A **postcard** is a small card that can be sent in the mail. People write short notes on postcards. People often send postcards when they are on a trip. Postcards are mailed without envelopes. You can write the address and message, and then place a stamp right on the postcard.

Here is a postcard that Little Critter wrote to his friend Tiger.

July 7, 2002

Dear Tiger,
   I am having a cool time this summer. My family went to Critter World. I went on the Spider three times. I wish we could go on it together — just you and me!
      Your friend,
      Little Critter

Tiger
23 North Street
Critterville, U.S.A.

The other side of the postcard looks like this:

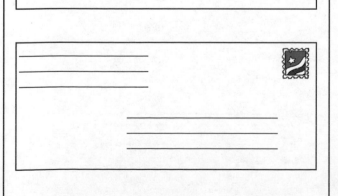

Just Practicing: Writing Postcards

Here are some blank postcards for you to write. Don't forget that the message goes on the left side, and the address goes on the right side.

message   address

Answers will vary.

SPECTRUM

SPECTRUM WORKBOOKS
ILLUSTRATED BY MERCER MAYER!

Grades K–2 • 128–160 full-color pages • Size: 8.375" x 10.875" • Paperback

McGraw-Hill, the premier educational publisher for grades PreK–12, and acclaimed children's author and illustrator, Mercer Mayer, are the proud creators of this workbook line featuring the lovable Little Critter. Like other Spectrum titles, the length, breadth, and depth of the activities in these workbooks enable children to learn a variety of skills about a single subject.

- Mercer Mayer's Little Critter family of characters has sold over 50 million books. These wholesome characters and stories appeal to both parents and teachers.
- Each full-color workbook is based on highly respected McGraw-Hill Companies' textbooks.
- All exercises feature easy-to-follow instructions.
- An answer key is included in each workbook.

Wholesome, well-known characters
plus proven school curriculum
equals learning success!

TITLE	ISBN	PRICE
LANGUAGE ARTS		
Grade K	1-57768-840-6	$8.95
Grade 1	1-57768-841-4	$8.95
Grade 2	1-57768-842-2	$8.95
MATH		
Grade K	1-57768-800-7	$8.95
Grade 1	1-57768-801-5	$8.95
Grade 2	1-57768-802-3	$8.95
PHONICS		
Grade K	1-57768-820-1	$8.95
Grade 1	1-57768-821-X	$8.95
Grade 2	1-57768-822-8	$8.95
READING		
Grade K	1-57768-810-4	$8.95
Grade 1	1-57768-811-2	$8.95
Grade 2	1-57768-812-0	$8.95
SPELLING		
Grade K	1-57768-830-9	$8.95
Grade 1	1-57768-831-7	$8.95
Grade 2	1-57768-832-5	$8.95
WRITING		
Grade K	1-57768-850-3	$8.95
Grade 1	1-57768-851-1	$8.95
Grade 2	1-57768-852-X	$8.95

Prices subject to change without notice.

Coming in June 2003!

TITLE	ISBN	PRICE
PRESCHOOL		
Basic Concepts	1-57768-509-1	$8.95
Letters and Sounds	1-57768-539-3	$8.95
Numbers and Counting	1-57768-519-9	$8.95
Reading Readiness	1-57768-529-6	$8.95
Beginning Math	1-57768-579-2	$8.95
Beginning Phonics	1-57768-589-X	$8.95
Beginning Reading	1-57768-599-7	$8.95
Beginning Writing	1-57768-549-0	$8.95

Prices subject to change without notice.

SPECTRUM

Brought to you by McGraw-Hill, the premier educational publisher for grades PreK–12.
All our workbooks meet school curriculum guidelines and correspond to
The McGraw-Hill Companies' classroom textbooks.

LANGUAGE ARTS

Grades 3–6 • 160 full-color pages
Size: 8.375" x 10.875" • Paperback

Encourages creativity and builds confidence by making writing fun! Sixty four-part lessons strengthen writing skills by focusing on parts of speech, word usage, sentence structure, punctuation, and proofreading. This series is based on the highly respected SRA/McGraw-Hill language arts series. Answer key included.

TITLE	ISBN	PRICE
LANGUAGE ARTS		
Gr. 3	1-57768-483-4	$8.95
Gr. 4	1-57768-484-2	$8.95
Gr. 5	1-57768-485-0	$8.95
Gr. 6	1-57768-486-9	$8.95
MATH		
Gr. K	1-57768-400-1	$8.95
Gr. 1	1-57768-401-X	$8.95
Gr. 2	1-57768-402-8	$8.95
Gr. 3	1-57768-403-6	$8.95
Gr. 4	1-57768-404-4	$8.95
Gr. 5	1-57768-405-2	$8.95
Gr. 6	1-57768-406-0	$8.95
Gr. 7	1-57768-407-9	$8.95
Gr. 8	1-57768-408-7	$8.95
PHONICS (Grades K–3)/WORD STUDY and PHONICS (Grades 4–6)		
Gr. K	1-57768-450-8	$8.95
Gr. 1	1-57768-451-6	$8.95
Gr. 2	1-57768-452-4	$8.95
Gr. 3	1-57768-453-2	$8.95
Gr. 4	1-57768-454-0	$8.95
Gr. 5	1-57768-455-9	$8.95
Gr. 6	1-57768-456-7	$8.95
READING		
Gr. K	1-57768-460-5	$8.95
Gr. 1	1-57768-461-3	$8.95
Gr. 2	1-57768-462-1	$8.95
Gr. 3	1-57768-463-X	$8.95
Gr. 4	1-57768-464-8	$8.95
Gr. 5	1-57768-465-6	$8.95
Gr. 6	1-57768-466-4	$8.95

Prices subject to change without notice.

MATH

Grades K–8 • Over 150 pages
Size: 8.375" x 10.875" • Paperback

Features easy-to-follow instructions that give students a clear path to success. This series includes comprehensive coverage of the basic skills, helping children master math fundamentals. Answer key included.

PHONICS/WORD STUDY

Grades K–6 • Over 200 pages
Size: 8.375" x 10.875" • Paperback

Provides everything children need to build multiple skills in language arts. This series focuses on phonics, structural analysis, and dictionary skills, and offers creative ideas for using phonics and word study skills in language areas. Answer key included.

READING

Grades K–6 • Over 150 full-color pages
Size: 8.375" x 10.875" • Paperback

This full-color series creates an enjoyable reading environment, even for below-average readers. Each book contains captivating content, colorful characters, and compelling illustrations, so children are eager to find out what happens next. Answer key included.

SPELLING

Grades 3–6 • 160 full-color pages
Size: 8.375" x 10.875" • Paperback

This full-color series links spelling to reading and writing, and increases skills in words and meanings, consonant and vowel spellings, and proofreading practice. Speller dictionary and answer key included.

VOCABULARY

Grades 3–6 • 160 full-color pages
Size: 8.375" x 10.875" • Paperback

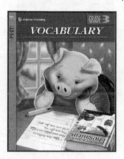

An essential building block for writing and reading proficiency, this series extends vocabulary knowledge through grade-appropriate instruction and activities. Synonyms, antonyms, homophones, word families, and word forms are among the key concepts explored. Instruction is based on language arts and reading standards, offering a solid foundation for language arts, spelling, and reading comprehension. The series features a proficiency test practice section for standards-aligned assessment. Answer key included.

WRITING

Grades 3–6 • 160 full-color pages
Size: 8.375" x 10.875" • Paperback

Lessons focus on creative and expository writing using clearly stated objectives and pre-writing exercises. Eight essential reading skills are applied. Activities include main idea, sequence, comparison, detail, fact and opinion, cause and effect, making a point, and point of view. Each book includes a Writer's Handbook that offers writing tips. Answer key included.

TEST PREP

Grades 1–8 • 160 full-color pages
Size: 8.375" x 10.875" • Paperback

This series teaches the skills, strategies, and techniques necessary for students to succeed on any standardized test. Each book contains guidelines and advice for parents along with study tips for students. Grades 1 and 2 cover Reading, Language Arts, Writing, and Math. Grades 3 through 8 cover Reading, Language Arts, Writing, Math, Social Studies, and Science.

FLASH CARDS

Card size: 3.0625" x 4.5625"

Flash cards provide children with one of the most effective ways to drill and practice fundamentals. The cards have large type, making it easy for young learners to read them. Each pack contains 50 flash cards, including a parent instruction card that offers suggestions for fun, creative activities and games that reinforce children's skills development.

TITLE	ISBN	PRICE
SPELLING		
Gr. 3	1-57768-493-1	$8.95
Gr. 4	1-57768-494-X	$8.95
Gr. 5	1-57768-495-8	$8.95
Gr. 6	1-57768-496-6	$8.95
VOCABULARY		
Gr. 3	1-57768-793-0	$8.95
Gr. 4	1-57768-794-9	$8.95
Gr. 5	1-57768-795-7	$8.95
Gr. 6	1-57768-796-5	$8.95
WRITING		
Gr. 3	1-57768-913-5	$8.95
Gr. 4	1-57768-914-3	$8.95
Gr. 5	1-57768-915-1	$8.95
Gr. 6	1-57768-916-X	$8.95
TEST PREP		
Gr. 1–2	1-57768-662-4	$9.95
Gr. 3	1-57768-663-2	$9.95
Gr. 4	1-57768-664-0	$9.95
Gr. 5	1-57768-665-9	$9.95
Gr. 6	1-57768-666-7	$9.95
Gr. 7	1-57768-667-5	$9.95
Gr. 8	1-57768-668-3	$9.95
FLASH CARDS		
Addition	1-57768-167-3	$2.99
Alphabet	1-57768-151-7	$2.99
Division	1-57768-158-4	$2.99
Money	1-57768-150-9	$2.99
Multiplication	1-57768-157-6	$2.99
Numbers	1-57768-127-4	$2.99
Phonics	1-57768-152-5	$2.99
Sight Words	1-57768-160-6	$2.99
Subtraction	1-57768-168-1	$2.99
Telling Time	1-57768-138-X	$2.99

Prices subject to change without notice.

FIRST READERS

MERCER MAYER FIRST READERS
SKILLS AND PRACTICE

Levels 1, 2, 3 (Grades PreK–2) • 24 Pages • Size: 6" x 9" • Paperback

Young readers will enjoy these simple and engaging stories written with their reading level in mind. Featuring Mercer Mayer's charming illustrations and favorite Little Critter characters, these are the books children will want to read again and again. To ensure reading success, the First Readers are based on McGraw-Hill's respected educational SRA Open Court Reading Program. Skill-based activities in the back of the book also help reinforce learning. A word list is included for vocabulary practice. Each book contains 24 full-color pages.

Level 1 (Grades PreK–K)

TITLE	ISBN	PRICE
Camping Out	1-57768-806-6	$3.95
No One Can Play	1-57768-804-X	$3.95
Play Ball	1-57768-803-1	$3.95
Snow Day	1-57768-805-8	$3.95
Little Critter Slipcase 1	1-57768-823-6	$15.95
(Contains 4 titles; 1 each of the above titles)		
Show and Tell	1-57768-835-X	$3.95
New Kid in Town	1-57768-829-5	$3.95
Country Fair	1-57768-827-9	$3.95
My Trip to the Zoo	1-57768-826-0	$3.95
Little Critter Slipcase 2	1-57768-853-8	$15.95
(Contains 4 titles; 1 each of the above titles)		

Level 2 (Grades K–1)

TITLE	ISBN	PRICE
The Mixed-Up Morning	1-57768-808-2	$3.95
A Yummy Lunch	1-57768-809-0	$3.95
Our Park	1-57768-807-4	$3.95
Field Day	1-57768-813-9	$3.95
Little Critter Slipcase 1	1-57768-824-4	$15.95
(Contains 4 titles; 1 each of the above titles)		
Beach Day	1-57768-844-9	$3.95
The New Fire Truck	1-57768-843-0	$3.95
A Day at Camp	1-57768-836-8	$3.95
Tiger's Birthday	1-57768-828-7	$3.95
Little Critter Slipcase 2	1-57768-854-6	$15.95
(Contains 4 titles; 1 each of the above titles)		

Level 3 (Grades 1–2)

TITLE	ISBN	PRICE
Surprise!	1-57768-814-7	$3.95
Our Friend Sam	1-57768-815-5	$3.95
Helping Mom	1-57768-816-3	$3.95
My Trip to the Farm	1-57768-817-1	$3.95
Little Critter Slipcase 1	1-57768-825-2	$15.95
(Contains 4 titles; 1 each of the above titles)		
Grandma's Garden	1-57768-846-5	$3.95
Class Trip	1-57768-845-7	$3.95
Goodnight, Little Critter	1-57768-834-1	$3.95
Our Tree House	1-57768-833-3	$3.95
Little Critter Slipcase 2	1-57768-855-4	$15.95
(Contains 4 titles; 1 each of the above titles)		

Prices subject to change without notice.

The Children's Book Council has named **Snow Day** and **Our Friend Sam** recipients of the Council's "Children's Choices 2002" awards, placing the two titles among the highest recommended books for children.